THE
AMERICAN
STORE
WINDOW

THE AMERICAN STORE WINDOW

BY LEONARD S. MARCUS

WHITNEY LIBRARY OF DESIGN
an imprint of Watson-Guptill Publications/New York

The Architectural Press Ltd./London

FRONTISPIECE

Howard Nevelow, Delman Shoe Salon, New York, 1968. Photograph by Malan Studio, Inc., New York. Courtesy Delman Shoe Salon.

PHOTOGRAPHY CREDITS

Photographers' works are cited by illustration number.

Bill Bernardo, Jr.: 127, 132, 135
Chicago Architectural Photographing Co., David R. Phillips: 27
Davis: 45–47, 49–58, 143–144
Fifth Ave. Display Photographers, New York: 105–106
Malan Studio, Inc., New York: 23–26, 43, 59–86, 88–104, 107–108, 110–121, 145
Morton: 17
Virginia Roehl: 11, 13, 16, 28–36, 42, 44
Skelton Studios: 48
Fred Stein, Copyright Fred Stein: 15
Whittington: 18
Worsinger: 3–6, 8–10, 12, 14, 21–22, 131

SOURCES

Illustration sources are cited by illustration number.

The Norman Bel Geddes Collection at the Hoblitzelle Theatre Arts Library, Humanities Research Center, The University of Texas at Austin, by permission of the executrix of the Norman Bel Geddes estate, Edyth Lutyens Bel Geddes: 2
Robert Benzio: 104
Bergdorf Goodman: 120
Bill Bernardo, Jr.: 127, 132, 135
Bloomingdale's: 122–123, 125–126
Bonwit Teller: 6, 8–10, 13, 28–30, 32, 34–36, 39–40, 80–81, 146–151
Carson Pirie Scott & Co.: 20
Delman Shoe Salon: 82–86, 88–94
The Emporium: 17
Gump's: 45–58
I. Magnin: 128
I. Miller Shoes: 121, 145
Sarah Tomerlin Lee: 7, 11–12, 14

Liberty House: 143–144
S. Liebmann: 16
Lord & Taylor: 4–5, 21–26, 65–66, 108, 114, 131
Gene McCabe: 95–103, 113
William Foxall Mac Elree, Jr.: 67–68, 110–112
Marshall Field & Co.: 1, 19, 27
Malan Studio, Inc., New York: 38, 42–43, 69–79, 115–119
Gene Moore: 31, 33, 37, 41
Howard Nevelow: 44
Dana O'Clare: 3
David M. O'Grady: 136
Saks Fifth Avenue: 59–64, 105–107
Maggie Spring, 134, 137, 152–153
L. Stein: 15
Steuben Glass: 124
Whittington: 18
ZCMI: 138–142

First published 1978 in New York by Whitney Library of Design,
an imprint of Watson-Guptill Publications,
a division of Billboard Publications, Inc.,
1515 Broadway, New York, N.Y. 10036

Library of Congress Cataloging in Publication Data

Marcus, Leonard S. 1950–
   The American store window.
   Bibliography: pp.204–205
   Includes index.
   1.   Show-windows—United States—History.   I.   Title.
HF5845.M35   1978   659.1′57   78-18176
ISBN 0-8230-7030-1

First published 1978 in Great Britain by The Architectural Press Ltd.,
9 Queen Anne's Gate, London SW1H 9BY
ISBN 85139-041-2

Edited by Sarah Bodine and Susan Davis
Designed by James Craig and Bob Fillie
Composed in 12 point Bodoni Book

HF
5845
M35
1978

CONTENTS

FOREWORD
A Conversation
with Gene Moore

Marcus: You talk about designing windows as being like a reporter.

Moore: What I mean by that is to try to be aware of everything that is going on in the world. And there are many things that happen that I think are important enough to try to do something about visually in display. For instance, the newspaper strike we had in New York some years ago. The water shortage. The transit strike we had in New York. Things like that. If you can do it and treat it with humor it gets across to people and it's great fun to do, too. When the transit strike happened, I went over to a toy store and got all sorts of modes of transportation other than subway and bus, like skates, a bicycle, unicycle, pogo stick, and put them in the windows. The public loved it. It gives them something to laugh about, about a situation that is not funny.

Marcus: Unusual display is often limited to fashion, but recently I have noticed florists, bakeries, record stores trying to do something with their windows.

Moore: In Europe where they sell vegetables, even on pushcarts, they always make it look so beautiful. It would be fun to do windows in a hardware store. I could enjoy that for a short time. You have so much merchandise to work with. And I don't think you have to show it all, for God's sake. It would be much more fun if a hardware store did windows with ideas featuring one particular thing to make people stop and look and pay attention to it.

Marcus: Well, a hardware store is a place where people usually go when they need a specific thing, but you think it would make a difference?

Moore: It would start people talking about the store. And they would, if it went on week after week. It becomes an identification with that particular store. After all, you wash your face every day and try to look as attractive as you possibly can. And it is your face. And it's very important to try to make it as attractive as you can.

Marcus: Do you think that in some sense people also see themselves when they look in a store window? What do they see?

Moore: Well, I think people like to have an association with what they see. I think there's a lot of fantasizing that goes on in people's minds when they look at things. They may not even tell themselves about it directly, but I think subconsciously it's there.

Marcus: Is that mainly an enjoyable experience, do you think?

Moore: Yes, I think it's an enjoyable experience, exactly as people see things in windows that revolt them. That works just the opposite way. It's amazing what different views you can get on the same window. I remember once at Bonwit's I had a set of back-to-school windows. The whole floor was covered with college textbooks. No floor showing, just textbooks. I went into Window Four, and there was a medical book and I opened it up and all of a sudden there were drawings of the female parts. I thought, "Oh, that's interesting," so I had that in. I got a call the next day from the president of the store saying, "That window you have—I got a call from this woman and she is in-*sulted*." Christ, it didn't occur to me that it could offend anybody, that anybody would look to find something like that and be incensed about it. So I said, "Okay, I'll change it." So I went into the window (I knew *exactly* where it was). So I started looking through the book and I found drawings of the male parts. So I opened it to that and I left that in. Nobody said a word. Crazy. . . .

Marcus: Do you enjoy living in New York?

Moore: Oh, yes, I knew I could never, ever accomplish anything I wanted to in the South. I just couldn't. This city is so receptive to everything, to ideas. It's a challenge. The whole city's a challenge. For God's sake, just walking down the street's a challenge. Here nothing stifles you.

Marcus: Display at most stores is primarily a form of direct advertising. Do you see much advertising apart from display that you think is well done?

Moore: Very little. How many television commercials do you really remember? There are very few that make an impression on me. Morris the Cat. You certainly remember him. Even my cat remembers him. He loves to watch him on television. And the Alka-Seltzer thing. That is really marvelous. There aren't many. Some of the cosmetic ones are very bad, and the perfume ones. I can't think of one that I really remember. There is such a thing as being so *bad* that people remember you, too. There's that.

Marcus: I have seen some of the perfume ads that Marcel Vertès did for Schiaparelli around 1940.

Moore: They were so atmospheric. He was a marvelous painter. He really was. But today hardly anyone uses art work. They use people. Fashion magazines today are a bore from the cover all through to the end and particularly the cover. It's always a girl and you can hardly tell one girl from the other and you can't tell one magazine from the other except if you read the title. You can't just have a quick look and say, "That's *Vogue*, that's *Harper's*, that's whatever." They all look alike. Years ago they had marvelous artists that did covers. Vertès did some covers. Cassandra, who was a Spanish painter, did some covers. There were so many. They say it doesn't sell. Well, I don't know that that's true. I just don't believe it.

Marcus: You often work with scale in your windows, which gives them a fairytale quality. Are you interested in fairytales?

Moore: Oh, yes. I think anyone who isn't interested in fairytales hasn't lived. If I had my choice of doing something, I think I would like to do fairytales for children for TV. I think there are so many fairytales that kids of this time know nothing about. Almost all of us have our own fairytales in our own minds, but it's so nice to have them written down somewhere by someone who knew how to write, and to read them. I think fairytales have gone out of popularity somehow. It's a pity.

Marcus: Maybe it's because many young children now are made to be sophisticated. In fairytales it's often the simpleton who turns out to be wiser than everyone else.

Moore: Sophistication is something I don't understand.

Marcus: Really?

Moore: I don't understand it. There's so much artificiality in the word today. You either are sophisticated or you aren't, exactly as I think you either have taste and it can be developed or you have no taste and nothing can develop it. You can't hide what you are and what you are comes out in your work, in everything you do. I may have an idea of what I want to do before I go into a window, but then the subconscious takes over and you are doing things that your subconscious dictates that you don't think about. You can't. Who knows the subconscious? No one. . . .

Marcus: The Shadow knows. . . .

Moore: I think most likely he's the only one that does. There have to be some basics somewhere based on past history. You can't do anything and say, "That's great." Who says so? "I do, because I'm wearing it."

Marcus: Do you like to look at photographs of past displays?

Moore: I find it fascinating to look at pictures. So many wonderful things were done during the fifties. Henry Callahan was so marvelous. He really was wonderful. When it comes around the design, good design is good design, whether it is now or whether it was a hundred years ago or a hundred years from now. That doesn't change. It's almost a classic. There aren't many classics around today.

Marcus: I think there is a difference between commercialism and commercial art. That is, not all commercial art is commercial in a sense in that it's done to a certain high standard.

Moore: That's very true.

Marcus: That's what I've been interested in.

This book began nearly three years ago as an adventure when I learned that several stores around the country have maintained extensive photo archives of their past window displays and that much of the best material was unpublished. A few stores have saved pictures from as early as 1910. Many other stores keep no photographs of their windows.

One display director, while traveling, carried all the photographs of his work in a trunk, which he lost. A display director who thought his store's photo collection went back to 1929 found, on checking in his storeroom, that the oldest photos on file were from 1974. The other pictures had apparently been thrown away to make shelf space. Large photo collections were lost in fires—the photos of Guy and Thelma Malloy's work at Neiman-Marcus; the negatives of the New York photographer Worsinger. Some display photographers have kept tens of thousands of negatives, but in no particular order. Some display directors have kept no photos of their work. Nevertheless, photographs of a great deal of the best American display work of the last sixty years have somehow survived and remained accessible.

Originally taken for publicity purposes or as a designer's reference source or historical record, many of the photographs that I found appeared not to have been looked at for many years. They were often covered with dust, stored in out-of-the-way rooms, and so on. A few designers whom I met, however, have taken an interest in the older photos in their stores' files. At least three designers found ideas for their current work in older photos that turned up during the research for this book.

Some detective work was needed to locate certain of the pictures. The search for a photograph of a window by Salvador Dali (see page 109), for instance, led from a brief reference in a thirty-year-old, out-of-print book to a photo research center, to a foreign language institute, to a university personnel office, and then to an apartment in an outlying section of New York, where the negative is carefully filed.

To locate a photograph of display work by the industrial designer Norman Bel Geddes (see page 101), by contrast, only two phone calls and one letter were needed. Several designers suggested the names of others whom they thought might have interesting pictures. In this way, one source of material often led to another. Several stores and photographers made their complete files available to me. Others lent selections of photos. In all, nearly fifty thousand pictures were considered.

The photographs in this book are straightforward visual reports of the work of more than forty display directors, their assistants, and staffs. The pictures are not interpretations on the photographers' part. They do not, like the French photographer Atget's pictures of Paris shop windows, imply an attitude toward their subject.

My main criterion for choosing photographs has been excellence of design. Variety was also considered, as was historical interest. Only a very few pictures, though, were chosen because of their age or historical importance alone, and these are to be found among the pictures illustrating the Essay. The other photographs are of displays whose visual interest and purity of design are largely conveyed by the pictures.

A photograph of a well-designed thirties display may be of current value in most of the ways that a well-designed thirties dress, chair, or poster may be of value: as an object that is pleasing visually; as a source of ideas for contemporary designers; as evidence for historians and others interested in the ongoing evolution of style, fashion, popular culture, commercial art. The photographs document many relationships between display and developments in society, the fine arts, and the media, and I have tried in the Essay to describe these relationships as broadly as possible.

The photos also illustrate various patterns within display. Among the curious finds were photos of nearly identical windows designed at different stores twenty or more years apart—parallel solutions arrived at independently by talented designers (see pages 178 and 190).

Some designers who have done fine display work are not represented because their work was not known to me, or because no photographs could be found of their windows, or because little or no information could be found about their careers. Many photos of first-rate windows were omitted for lack of space. Each picture was chosen individually, without reference to store or designer.

In most but not all cases, the display director listed in the caption was also the designer of the display. Whenever possible, the actual designer is credited.   Photo credit was omitted only in the few cases where the store had no record. The names of a few of the early display directors also could not be found.

For permission to reproduce photographs I wish to thank the photographers, stores, and university libraries named in the captions.

Many people contributed to the completion of this project. I would like to acknowledge the help of Dan Arje, Laurence B. Bartscher, Edyth Lutyens Bel Geddes, Robert Benzio, J. M. Biow, Colin Birch, Emil A. Blasberg, Albert Bliss, Steve Brady, Mary Brosnan, Jon Brown, Jim Buckley, Henry F. Callahan, Janet Campbell, Frans Camps, Red Cat, Katherine Chettle, John Cocozza, W. H. Crain, Robert Currie, Maria DeLuca, Marvin H. Dorfmann, John Fariello, Ron Feiman, Bobbi Fisher, Lester Gaba, Pamela Gramke, Buddy Haskins, Walter H. Herdeg, Victor Hugo, Nancy Kammer, Don Kane, Jane S. Kaufman, Peggy Kaufman, Sarah Tomerlin Lee, S. Liebmann, James L. Luker, Gene McCabe, Michael McCoy, Bill Mac Elree, Robert Mahoney, Mary Malan, Helen Marcus, Anthony L. Markus, Raymond Mastrobuoni, Bud Meads, Jerry Miller, Richard Minto, Gene Moore, Robert E. Moore, Ron Nelson, Howard Nevelow, Tom Nicoll, Dana O'Clare, David M. O'Grady, Tom Passarella, Candy Pratts, Jack Quinn, Bill Robbins, Ellen Fletcher Rosebrock, Robert F. Ruffino, Reed Schlademan, Jonathan Schonfeld, Judy Simonson, James Small, Ron Smith, Maggie Spring, Liselotte Stein, Frances Stelloff, Marvin Sylvor, Richard Thaxton, Jerry Thorne, Mallory Tone, Rita Weiss, Pat Weissberg, Bill Welch, the display staff of Marshall Field & Co., the staff of the New York Public Library

I would like especially to thank Dick Faust of ST Publications for his many helps; Michael Dunas of Watson-Guptill Publications and my editors Sarah Bodine and Susan Davis for their interest in this project; my parents and family for their encouragement.

ESSAY

The Wonderful Wizard of Oz has a curious place in the history of American window display. Its author, L. Frank Baum, was the founder and editor of *The Show Window,* the first display trade magazine. Baum, a former traveling salesman of glassware, had as editor also started up the first industry organization, The National Association of Window Trimmers of America, in 1898. Two years later, *The Wizard of Oz* had made him suddenly famous, and he resigned from the journal to write *Oz* sequels. That Baum saw a connection between window trimming, as window design work was then called, and his imaginative fiction is not definitely known, although in the magazine he does often cast his observations about display in the form of anecdotes and stories.

In one such tale, two public statues meet at a street corner after dark and begin talking about a mannequin they both can see in a shop window across the way. "She appears," the first statue tells the second statue, "at the lighting up of the window, and stands there looking, looking, looking straight ahead, like a bird of paradise under the spell of a serpent's jeweled eye." The second statue approaches the window for a closer look, but just then the lights of the statues, which permit them to see, are shut off for the night, leaving only the mannequin illuminated. "The angelic creature," Baum concludes, "posing within the window was a wax figure robed in fashion's most superbly shaped garb."

For Baum as a writer, *The Wizard of Oz* may well have represented an imaginative development beyond the all-too-perfect waxwork effigies of Victorian display. Baum's two public statues are close enough relations to The Straw Man and The Tin Man until, that is, the latter pair become fully human, finding a brain and heart for themselves in The Emerald City. Little Dorothy is not an angelic bird of paradise, but a plain Midwestern girl who gets swept away to the big city not by the weather, it turns out, but by the imagination.

Around 1900, when *The Wizard of Oz* first appeared, thousands of young Americans were leaving farms and small towns to live in cities. They left for a new life like that described in the national picture magazines, such as *Harper's* and *Collier's,* with their accounts and illustrations by Charles Dana Gibson and others of ambitious young men and polite but worldly Gibson Girls who had cast off the caged-bird loveliness of Baum's Victorian mannequin ideal.

Dorothy, in the *Oz* tale, does not reach The Emerald City by looking into a store window, but through a dream.

Yet in every American small town of 1900, certain shop windows, however awkwardly done they may at times have been, would have been constant reminders to the adventurous of the great cities with their finer things and their wider ranges of choices and opportunities of other kinds—cultural, social, spiritual—real and illusory.

The glittering imagery of The Emerald City at least suggests that the material and spiritual attractions of cities were, in Baum's mind, not entirely separable. American cities of 1900 were becoming cultural as well as commercial centers. The cities' principal streets, lined with office buildings, hotels, theaters, and department stores took on increasingly substantial airs of granite, marble, iron, gold leaf and glass.

People dressed up and went into town, where they became a part of the display or went about their business. People strolled, stopped at public fountains, went to restaurants, theaters, and parks, and window-shopped. In this way, the cities at their formal center became increasingly theatrical in style—places not only of business but of a kind of public performance. City store windows were and are a part of this urban attitude of display. And the best displaymen have often shown a quality of imagination and fantasy in their windows that is related on its own terms and within the context of both a store and city to *Oz.*

PREMODERN DISPLAY

Merchandise display—which even in its simplest forms involves a basic concern for showing what one has to offer in the best possible light—is almost certainly as old as trade and commerce. Window display as we know it probably began in the northeastern United States around 1840. In England and France, window display was first widely experimented with during the 1860s and 1870s. In America Greek Revival store fronts with relatively large windows were built to replace Federal period shops, and merchants apparently decided to take advantage of the additional window space for display. Often open shelves were constructed behind the window glass, with objects placed behind each pane of the latticed window.

Both in Europe and in the United States, the first shops were for the most part extensions of the merchant's home. The traditional shop consisted either of a house in which a front room had been converted for commercial use or of a two- or three-story structure with the shopkeeper's living quarters on the building's upper floors. There was thus an interest in maintaining the privacy of the dwellers of these buildings that would have limited the possibilities for commercial window display. In Charles Dickens' *The Old Curiosity Shop,* which is set in London around 1840, the narrator seems very surprised to have found that a part of the shop's front door was "of glass unprotected by any shutter." Many of the first display windows, American or European, appear to have been shuttered for the night, although an English visitor to the United States, Anne Royall, wrote in her undated diary of the early 1800s that "at night the wealth and splendor of Philadelphia appears to the best advantage . . . the windows being lighted with numerous lamps and gaslights which with the lamps in the streets, and the lustre of the glittering wares in the windows, present a scene of astounding beauty."

The American Greek Revival stores of the 1830s were not house-and-shops, but strictly commercial buildings. As they appeared in New York and in other eastern cities and as the first serious interest was shown in window display, many merchants and tradesmen moved their families into houses at a distance from their places of business.

The pawnbroker's three-ball symbol and the apothecary's mortar and pestle are among the oldest examples of a type of commercial display that is believed to have had its origin in medieval Europe. Along American shopping streets of the early nineteenth century, a great collection of such shop devices and ornaments was to be seen.

Trade signs and symbols would have been an aid to those unable to read a printed signboard; even a hundred years ago this would have included a large percentage of the population. Carved wooden eagles, although not descriptive of the store, were also very popular in nineteenth-century America. And as handcrafted objects, these patriotic figures—like ships' figureheads, circus ornaments, and weathervanes that were also being made at about this time and like cigar store Indians and other stock display ornaments—might have had some peculiarity that made one more memorable than others of its kind. Hanging cutout signs of, say, an ostrich or an elephant, with their various appeals to a passerby's memory and imagination, were also frequently employed. In print ads, storeowners sometimes made reference to a decorative device in stating the shop address, as did the early nineteenth-century New York toy dealer "Smith Prentiss, at the Sign of the Golden Rose, 149 Broadway."

That such display emblems might lend a fantastic air to an ordinary shop and neighborhood was evident to Charles Dickens when he visited Boston in 1842. The city, where "the houses were so bright and gay, the signboards were painted in such gaudy colors, the gilded letters were so very golden, the bricks were so very red, . . . the knobs and plates upon the street-doors so marvelously bright and twinkling," seemed to Dickens to be "so slight and insubstantial" in appearance that it reminded him of stage sets for a pantomime. "It rarely happens in the business streets that a tradesman . . . resides above his store, so that many occupations are carried on in one house, and the whole front is covered with boards and inscriptions. As I walked along, I kept glancing up at these boards, confidently expecting to see them change into something; and I never turned a corner suddenly without looking out for the clown and pantaloon, who, I had no doubt, were hiding in a doorway or behind some pillar close at hand. As to Harlequin and Columbine, I discovered immediately that they lodged . . . at a very small clock-maker's, one story high, near the hotel; which, in addition to various symbols and devices, almost covering the whole front, had a great dial hanging out—to be jumped through, of course."

Most hanging shop symbols were banned by local ordinances in American cities and towns around the midnineteenth century, for much the same reason that streetcriers were banned or discouraged by the 1890s, in an effort to promote what some of the more established merchants considered a more dignified atmosphere on the main shopping streets. Of the standing display figures, cigar store Indians, with their distinctly American drawing appeal, were still to be seen here and there in the 1930s. Barbershop poles remain in large numbers today; once electrified, they proved to be effective eye-catchers even on a fast-moving modern city street. Some city shoemakers and locksmiths still display a hanging sign of a shoe or key, now often outlined in neon. Pawnbroker's symbols have perhaps changed the least of all over hundreds of years.

As for American window display, once the precedent was established for showing merchandise through the glass, a shopkeeper with a feeling for decor or for dressing—both of which are types of display—may have experimented with different arrangements of materials, colors, and forms in a window. While shop signs and symbols usually only identified the type of goods available in a store (as well as perhaps whether the owner had a sense of humor), window display eventually became a means of articulating specific qualities of the store and its merchandise. Window display was thus not only more informative than the symbols, but also represented more of an attempt at direct salesmanship or persuasion, and in turn reflected basic developments in midnineteenth-century American society and economy: its increasing wealth and the increasing competitiveness of many of its people for a share of the wealth. As more merchandise, especially luxury goods, became available in midnineteenth-century stores, people more commonly went to stores not only to fill a specific need, as had usually been the case previously, but also merely to browse as a diversion or to window-shop.

Attractive window display seems at first to have been equated with displays of quantity. Some merchants apparently felt that the more merchandise they put in their windows, the less space was wasted, while other shopkeepers filled their display windows as a conspicuous show of material wealth and pride in abundance.

Anne Royall, a European visitor to Philadelphia in the early 1800s, found "the profusion of merchandise which lines the streets and windows . . . incredible." "The stores are gorged with goods," wrote another foreign visitor to Boston at about the time Charles Dickens was there, "so much so as to literally ooze out at doors and windows . . . from the upper windows stream whole pieces of flaring calico and gauzy ribbons. . . ."

During the nineteenth century, displays of apparently unlimited plenty, not only where merchandise was concerned, seemed to many observers, both foreign and American, to somehow represent an American national trait or habit. Charles Dickens found in New York (more so than in Boston) " a spirit of contention in reference to appearances, and the display of wealth and costly living." William Cobbett in 1817 remarked that at American dinner tables where he was a guest, "You are not much pressed to eat and drink, but such an abundance is spread before you . . . that you instantly lose all restraint." Marble palaces were built along Fifth Avenue in New York and then demolished ten years later as the city spread northward. Even obesity was said to be considered a symbol of prosperity by Americans. When in 1905 Andrew Carnegie gave money for the building of public libraries, *The New York World* embellished its report of the fact by observing that if "laid in a row on their edges with flat surfaces touching, this number of silver dollars [38 million] would extend . . . within two miles of the distance from New York to Philadelphia"—a single detail blown up to monumentality. But this was the idea of premodern display.

FIRST MODERN DEVELOP- MENTS

Around 1900, as many Americans moved away from rural areas to larger towns and cities, hundreds of regional and national organizations were formed through which people could relate to each other socially, economically, and politically. A great variety of professional groups were founded or given new life. The American Medical Association reorganized in 1901; the National Education Association did so in 1905. Most state bar associations were chartered between 1894 and 1916. So many local and regional chambers of commerce and boards of trade cropped up starting in 1884 that the U.S. Chamber of Commerce was founded in 1912 to coordinate them all. Labor unions attempted to form, although with more difficulty than the professional groups. As urbanization made retailing for the first time a bigger business than the wholesale—general-store type of distribution, which Marshall Field, for one, had previously considered the main part of his operation, retailers associations formed around the country, often quite suddenly. Retailing required some kind of merchandise display. Window trimmers appeared and multiplied. And it was in this hectic and, on the whole, promising atmosphere that The National Association of Window Trimmers of America under L. Frank Baum came into existence.

In 1907, at least three schools for window trimmers existed in Chicago and New York, and throughout the country, local and regional trimmers clubs formed for the exchange of ideas and for morale-boosting. *The Show Window* had changed hands, becoming *The Merchants Record and Show Window* in 1903. Prizes were awarded by the magazine for trimming excellence, and an annual national convention was held in Chicago.

In "The Science of Display," a prize-winning essay for 1910, trimmer T. K. Harveson remarked that "windows of a good many years ago . . . gave the impression of a side show at a circus, and the large flaming show cards of the 'barker' who stands outside urging you in." One wonders how reassured trimmers around the country were to learn that the low-paying and otherwise disparaged craft they were engaged in was in fact a science. Other trimmers insisted with equal conviction that display was an art.

Few skilled trades and professions did not have spokesmen making one or both claims—art or science—for their work around 1900. Such assertions, apart from whatever truth there may have been in them, were probably typical of a competitive society in which individuals increasingly identified themselves by their occupation rather than by their family, religion, or locality. Each working group wanted to claim as much authority and prestige for itself as possible. As for display, knowledge was at least becoming more refined and more systematized at this time, largely through the work of the various trimmers groups and *The Merchants Record*.

The carnival side of display, which trimmer Harveston had proudly stated was a thing of the past, was nevertheless still being seen at many stores. In an ad of 1910, a Buffalo, New York, display house offered "moving attractions . . . display tables, Ferris wheels, and merry-go-rounds." Around 1910 a popular type of display that was sometimes called "artistic," but which often also had the slightly musty look and regalia of a traveling sideshow, consisted of an elaborate tableau or model built entirely of some small item of merchandise—containers of salt, for instance, or boxes of a certain brand of cracker—used as building blocks. A favorite subject of these displays, which often had moving parts, was the clock—reminiscent of large floral clocks still seen today in some parks and gardens. Window trimmers, who at this time often worked with artificial flowers as their one and only prop, may have admired, and probably also designed, numerous such public display ornaments apart from their store work. The local pageantry of American town life would have afforded many opportunities for a talented trimmer to employ his skills. *The Merchants Record* reported in 1910 that "In hundreds of towns and cities throughout the U.S., during the summer months, there are held Home Comings, Carnivals, Anniversary Weeks, and Fourth of July celebrations. . . . Floral parades of decorated autos and floats are very popular. . . ." The Rose Parade is among today's outstanding survivals. Bunting and the American flag were also much commoner sights around 1910 than currently, and probably no type of window display showed more skill or familiarity with materials than did the patriotic displays in which nearly any kind of merchandise would be sold by stores on occasion.

An example of stocky window display from The Emporium in San Francisco in 1933, this window was designed with the elaborate finickiness of the early 1900s mechanical displays and with the energetic hyperbole of a Busby Berkeley dance routine. Photograph by Morton. Courtesy The Emporium.

In general, though, print advertising was considered around 1910 to be a much more effective selling medium than window display. Some shopkeepers used their windows as walls on which to display advertising posters. If merchandise was shown, the tendency was to make the trim "stocky," that is, to line up row after row of goods packed in tightly. The windows, in effect, were treated as three-dimensional catalogs.

The first efforts towards a more systematic approach to display were, as a result, modeled on developments in print advertising. When a writer in *The Merchants Record* wanted to discredit the concept of the "mixed display" (based on the idea that by assembling a great variety of goods in a window you would be sure to have something for everyone), he did so with reference to standard copywriting theory: "There are so many different articles making equal claims to notice that the observer is not appreciably impressed by any of them. . . . The two kinds of display may be compared to an advertisement that reads 'Groceries for Sale,' and one that exploits some particular line with descriptions and prices." *The Merchants Record* also gave special emphasis to the modern "show card"—the written message placed inside the display window—and ran articles on the design of print advertising itself.

Around 1910, the trend in print ads was towards less copy and more white space, with more room allowed for illustrations. The shift in balance towards pictures over words was favored for at least two reasons. A picture could be read faster than a long printed message, and such ads were also said to be more "artistic." The art and science of display were about to cross paths! In three dimensions, an artistic window display came to be considered one which, among other things, was not stocky. The show card became smaller, more concise, less ornamented. A few items of merchandise were, at least occasionally, left to stand in relief in a window as their own illustration.

With this development, distinctions about the best way of displaying different types of merchandise were also starting to be more precisely drawn. Less expensive types of goods were mainly left in catalog-style displays, which are still seen in stores in almost any town and city. But although experiments with the removal of clutter from windows were limited for the most part to displays of fashion, these efforts led window display in general to become more distinct from the print media. Trimmers working with a relatively small number of objects in a display became more aware of the conditions of the window space itself— scale, shape, background textures and materials, its three-dimensionality—as potentially dramatic and graphic elements. And this awareness, as *The Merchants Record* repeatedly observed, might have implications for displays of any type of merchandise, even when the window was made relatively stocky.

Another development in both the science and art of display concerned lighting. In "A Brilliantly Lighted Window," a *Merchants Record* article of 1910 that is remarkable now for its tone of discovery, improved night lighting was related to attracting the relatively new, urban middle class to stores in the evening: "Today . . . merchants realize that . . . hundreds of men and women who are busy all day must do their shopping after dark, and that there has grown up a large class known as 'window shoppers' who study the display windows after supper, comparing qualities and prices and making up their mind where to do their purchasing. . . ."

About 1910, silver-plated reflectors became available to focus the light of the recently developed Tungsten display lamp. Talented trimmers then had some means of achieving limited dramatic lighting effects. A new kind of specialist, the "illuminating engineer," advised progressive store managers both on display window fixturing and on the store's often hugely inefficient interior lighting arrangements. Nevertheless, in 1910 it was reported from New York that "in the large cities, many merchants consider that a window cannot be too brilliantly illuminated"—the principle of stock display, in effect, also applied to lighting. (Many store managers still take this attitude today.) In 1914, though, *The Merchants Record,* which four years earlier had written admiringly of a furniture concern in New Jersey that claimed its window was the "brightest in the world," cautioned: "The lighting must be the proper color; there must be just enough of it, neither too little nor too much — and it must be distributed just where it is needed. . . . Employ an expert. . . ."

Talented trimmers may have understood certain basic principles of display long before they had the authority to put them to use. Around 1910, most store managers lacked confidence in window trimming as a profession. In 1911, for instance, a leading trimmer from Dallas who, in an essay called "Stocky vs. Artistic Displays," argued that "high class goods . . . cannot be crowded in a window," added matter-of-factly that "it would be amazing news that any window trimmer dictates the display policy of his house." Since management gave its buyers full responsibility for sales, he explained, the buyers alone had the right to control merchandise presentation.

That same year, though, some New York City trimmers began systematically to "gauge the success of their windows by the amount of sales of stock they have featured in their window"—a survey method that is still used today. A Minneapolis writer on "The Status of the Decorator" noted in 1913 that "there are twice as many window dressers today holding good positions as there were ten years ago," although he found it necessary to add, ruefully but hopefully, that "in years gone by we have all heard of window dressers referred to as a drunken, irresponsible, lazy lot. Occasionally we hear it now but not so often. . . ." The next year, at the seventeenth annual Chicago convention, the trade group renamed itself "The International Association of Display Men" (IADM) — a "shorter and more comprehensive one than the old title," it was declared. Simultaneously, a campaign was launched to have "he who would and does accomplish beautiful and artistic window displays" no longer called a "trimmer" but a "display man."

The annual convention's format had been extended in 1912 to include not only social gatherings and readings of technical papers but also an "exhibition of all the fixtures, tools, materials, and decorative specialties" then available. This would have included onyx paper, which, in various patterns of onyx and marble, gave displaymen with a grandiose bent an inexpensive material with which to simulate classical decor in window settings. Felt, as a background material, was first introduced at about this time. And in 1911, "an extremely attractive and life-like figure for window display" was put on the market, after years of mannequins being considered in bad taste and dress forms with white paper cones in place of heads generally used in windows. In all, the first inventory of the national convention seems to have astonished the participants.

Just when the new wax mannequins became available, live models were also being used in the windows of many stores for scheduled fashion shows and day-long demonstrations by a tailor, for instance, to show how a garment for sale in the store was made. By 1914, though, the fancier stores decided that this sideshow type of display was undignified. Meanwhile the new "high class wax figures" gained wide acceptance among displaymen around the country. Mannequins, store managers noted, did not have to be paid.

Live models, like almost any source of motion in a window— mechanical props included not only cracker box clocks and revolving turntables but also flashing lights and at least one mannequin that rolled its eyes—almost always drew a crowd. These devices were the more or less awkward first attempts at coming to terms with a basic idea about display: that a window should "impress one with a feeling of life." To this remark, J. Clarence Bodine, a Chicago painter who pioneered in the design of decorative background panels for display, added that the modern store window should also look "neat, clean-cut, and snappy." A "feeling of life," Bodine and others suggested, could be achieved through simplicity of design and by applying artistic rather than heavily mechanical means.

By 1910, at least two American display directors had gained reputations for display work of unusual beauty. Visitors from Cairo, Illinois, and elsewhere to Chicago's Marshall Field caught glimpses of the splendor of ancient Cairo, Athens, and Rome in the window displays of Arthur V. Fraser. Fraser was the first displayman to be given an unlimited budget by his store. At Altman's in New York, Herman Frankenthal became known for his experiments with elegantly draped fabrics. His work was studied around the country and in Europe.

Despite such accomplishments, however, most window display before the late twenties remained fairly dull, without much fantasy, drama, or emotion. In 1919, *The Merchants Record* modernized its own format, probably reflecting the hope that numerous display resources—ideas, equipment, techniques, and materials—developed during twenty years of experimentation would soon be put into general use.

1919–1925

In 1919, Raymond Loewy arrived in New York City from France and found his first job with Macy's display department. Loewy had no experience as a displayman. He disliked the stocky and otherwise monotonous windows that he saw around the city and decided for his own first window to try an experiment.

Loewy used only one mannequin in a black evening gown with an extravagant fur spread at its feet and various accessories, as he described, "scattered around. . . . Instead of the usual blaze of diffused floodlights, I left the window in semidarkness. The only illumination came from three powerful spotlights focused on the figure. The result was a contrast of violent highlights and shadows. It was dramatic, simple, potent. It sang. . . . When I returned the following morning to see the results my boss was in the window huffing and puffing. . . ." Rather than be fired, Loewy resigned that day.

What was really new about Loewy's window was not the lack of clutter but the attitude of casual suggestiveness, a piquant contrast to the stately calm and sobriety that were hallmarks of the best display work until then. Loewy's window, like certain displays of the late thirties and the early seventies, was by contrast meant to shock. Loewy later did displays for Saks Fifth Avenue and, as is more generally known, designed a great variety of other large and small industrial and commercial projects, among them The Broadway Limited Train, an International Harvester cream separator, and the Chrysler Motors Pavilion at the 1939 World's Fair. It has often been overlooked that the industrial designers, among whom Loewy was a leader from the late twenties on, considered window display as apt a concern of modern design as were the products in the windows and the buildings themselves of which the windows were a part. Display, to these designers, represented a vehicle for streamlining the process of making industry's products rapidly known to the public. As the design theorist Frederick Kiesler wrote in 1930: "The evolution of the show window is due to one fact: speed. For this reason the show window is a modern method of communication."

A second American display trade journal, *Display World,* began publication in 1922, and in 1938, *The Merchants Record* merged with it under the newer magazine's more expansive title. Certain efforts during the early 1920s at putting display on a more scientific footing were, one suspects, mere "window-dressing," with more than a hint of the carnival magician's sleight of hand. For example, one "lighting efficiency expert" from Chicago, after assuring readers that the level of lighting intensity required for any given window had been worked out "quite scientifically," advised only that displaymen always make their own windows "a little brighter" than their neighbors'. For the first time attention was being given in the journal to the importance of day as well as night display lighting and to various ways that white and tinted lights alter the apparent color of objects in a window and also suggest a mood in a display. In 1922, it was also noted that at the IADM's twenty-fifth anniversary convention, "art critics" attended along with merchants and advertising men. Displaymen were also urged at this time to echo the store's print advertising in their displays not only by showing the same merchandise but also by adapting elements of the print ads' graphic style in their windows.

By the early twenties, many nationally circulating magazines existed, photojournalism and movies had become accepted realities for most Americans, and the widespread influence of these media, which mainly originated in cities that attracted high levels of talent, implied an exacting standard of comparison for the visual style of shop windows around the country. Displaymen experimented with methods of graphically relating a local shop window to these imposing phenomena. Blow-ups of news photos were used as background panels, as were adaptations of syndicated cartoon strips such as Mutt & Jeff; display card lithographs were mass-produced to provide "uniformly beautiful and attention-getting window accessories." The lithographer, *Display World* reported, provided the features of displays and guaranteed to "every merchant who makes use of his services, whether in a crossroad store or palatial metropolitan house, the same standards of excellence."

By the early 1920s, it was mainly at the crossroad stores that excellence in display work was in short supply. For the first time most Americans lived in cities. Smaller town merchandise displays and stores that were attempts at imitating their city counterparts more often than not merely provided further evidence that small town American life was economically and culturally declining. "'It's all very well to have modern lighting and a big display-space,'" remarks Raymie Wutherspoon, a local Gopher Prairie window-trimmer in Sinclair Lewis's *Main Street* of 1920, "'but when you get that in, you want to have some architecture too,'" a suggestion to which the store manager responded by putting in a cornice. "'Tin!' observed the traveling salesman.' . . . 'Well, what if it is tin?'" Raymie replies. "'That's not my fault. I told D.H. to make it polished granite. You make me tired!'"

Elsewhere in the novel, Lewis further illustrates the conflict of town and city values in an encounter between Carol, a city woman who has moved to Gopher Prairie, and Mrs. Swiftwaite at the latter's dress shop to which Carol has come to buy a new hat. The setting is actually a house-and-shop, a form which remained common in the smaller towns long after it had become impractical in the cities. "In the dingy old front parlor which she had tried to make smart with a pier glass, covers from fashion magazines, anemic French prints, Mrs. Swiftwaite moved smoothly among the dress-dummies and hat-rests, spoke smoothly as she took up a small black and red turban. 'I am sure the lady will find this extremely attractive.'

"'It's dreadfully tabby and small-towny,' thought Carol, while she soothed, 'I don't believe it quite goes with me.' . . . Carol studied the woman. She was as imitative as a glass diamond. She was the more rustic in her effort to appear urban. . . . Her skirt was hysterically checkered, her cheeks were too highly rouged. . . . Carol felt very condescending. . . . Carol was polite, and edged away, and went home unhappily. She was wondering whether her own airs were as laughable as Mrs. Swiftwaite's." At home, Carol looks in a mirror and finds to her despair that she herself has begun to look like a woman of Gopher Prairie, with "no flare of gaiety, no suggestion of cities, music, quick laughter. 'I have become a small town woman,'" she tells herself, "'modest and moral and safe. Protected from life.'" Lewis had as few illusions about city life as perhaps any American writer of this period. Thus he has Carol suspect that her own presumptions are as foolish as the shopkeeper's. But for Lewis, the city itself was a showplace that might at times amount only to falseness and self-deception but which also represented, to its credit, a "stately and permanent center." It stood, as if ineluctably, for life. It was in small towns such as Gopher Prairie, Lewis implies, that efforts at display, as gestures of worldliness, self-esteem, and pride, all but inevitably turned false or illusory.

The advent of the lithographed display card and of other mass-produced window trims that emanated from urban display manufacturers tended to level whatever eccentricities there were in local and regional styles of display. During the twenties, the window of odd or unusual interest, such as had once been seen in out-of-the-way places all around the country, increasingly became a phenomenon and an attraction of the cities. This trend, however, developed rather gradually. Each October, in Ypsilanti, Michigan, for instance, as late as 1927, the townspeople celebrated "window night," a special showing of seasonal merchandise in the local windows in conjunction with the fall "Corn and Canning Show." The window displays were done with autumn foliage, cornstalks, fruit, and flowers, and the streets themselves were festively decorated. At a similar window night in Davenport, Iowa, in 1928, a pageant was held in the school gymnasium. "The first scene," according to a local report, "opened with spring woods and an outing. In the interlude, the Imperial Male Quartet from Chicago sang. Scene two showed a modern city street, resembling a Central Park scene in New York. It depicted a spring rain, with shower rain drops in evidence by a special lighting effect. At this time, pupils of the Lend-a-Hand School of Dancing, under the direction of Miss L. Wilson, gave the 'Spring Shower Dance.'"

In New York and Chicago, the two leading American cities for display, interest in making windows modern-looking, or otherwise as visually arresting as other mass media imagery, was at most of the more

1927 drawing room scene from The Emporium in San Francisco is typical of fashion display at the more expensive stores, especially during the 1910s and 1920s. Deco display was a development away from this staid approach. Photograph by Morton. Courtesy The Emporium.

expensive stores cautiously modified by the idea that a fashion window ought to be a demonstration of conservative good taste. The American designer Norman Bel Geddes noted that during the early twenties, "the most generally used window background was a highly varnished paneling of yellow oak," reminiscent of a panelled drawing room or library. "The next most common background in use was an imitation stone, as cheerless and uninviting as a mausoleum." Much of the artistic effort consisted of refinements in the use of draperies, antique room furnishings, and potted plants in the staging of elaborate room settings.

A case of inspired fantasy nevertheless occasionally was shown in displays of fashion, as in a 1925 Lord & Taylor window of handkerchiefs. In designing this "exceptionally beautiful picture," *Display World* reported, a "Russian artist" spent three weeks making a reproduction of St. Patrick's Cathedral. More than two thousand cuts in compo board were needed for the detailing. It was placed on a low platform in the center of the window, the platform representing the sidewalk of the cathedral. "The showing of handkerchiefs was cleverly done by placing them on the steeples to have them suggest a slate type roofing. Others were draped all over the sides of the structure in neat designs forming a sort of framework for the prominent portions of the imitated stone work. Dolls made of handkerchiefs stood in the entrance ways and corridors. Other handkerchiefs and the store's handkerchief box of gay coloring were shown on low tables on either side of the cathedral finishing the floor." The store's management credited the display with having sold more than $5,000 worth of handkerchiefs in one day.

ART DECO DISPLAY

American displaymen had become used to thinking of their work as the most progressive in the world. In 1926, *Display World* noted with friendly but paternal interest that British displaymen had held their second annual trade convention and that trade groups had recently formed in Italy, South Africa, and Australia.

Most American display work had little if any relation to the abstract design and new materials in use at the Exposition des Arts Décoratifs et Industriels of 1925 in Paris. In fact, no American design work of any kind was represented in the show. *Display World* remained curiously silent about the event for most of 1926. Only an occasional ad, such as that for Yvonne Renet & Cie's "Parisienne millinery display heads," gave any hint in 1926 that the moderne or Art Deco style might affect the style and material resources of American window display.

Art Deco designers in Europe regarded the store window as a logical outlet for their program of merging fine and applied arts. A display might advertise the products of modern design, thus contributing to the process of the moving of goods, while doubling as a work of modern design in its own right or as an architectural ornament—an urban decorative and commercial art form.

The French artist and critic Ozenfant, who in general disparaged the decorative arts as frivolous nonsense, noted in 1931 that "Nowadays the window-dressing of small or great shops is very agreeable to see. A sane geometry derived from Purism and Léger directs the composition: dresses, boots, casseroles, all play their active parts in the equations to which they provide a solution. The art of window-dressing is an important factor in the town-planning to which Le Corbusier brought so much clear vision and power."

That American displaymen were willing, if only reluctantly, to learn from their European counterparts, is indicated by the fact that starting in late 1926, *Display World* gave considerable space to photographs of European moderne display windows, especially of German and Dutch examples. These European displays were thoroughly original in conception, rooted as they were in analogies to abstract poster graphics rather than to Victorian parlor melodrama, as was often the case with American windows. Decorative ornament was eliminated or kept to a minimum in the German and Dutch windows, and the idea of a display was boiled down to a single visual image.

At least one American designer was thinking along similar but independent lines at this time. The industrial designer Norman Bel Geddes was Franklin-Simon's display director in New York for two years during the late twenties. In his essay "In Window Display the Play's the Thing," he takes the still-contemporary attitude that "the store window is a stage on which the merchandise is presented as the

V. N. Siégel, the leading Deco mannequin designer, described his display figures as "fixtures" on which to hang clothes. Here in a 1930 window from H. C. Capwell Co. in Oakland, California, the so-called modern woman is seen at home in a modern world of Deco design. Courtesy H. C. Capwell Co.

actors. . . . The essential feature . . . is that it shall include nothing which serves only as decoration."

Bel Geddes built a permanent background for the store's windows, "the chief value of which was its unobtrusiveness in form and color. The structure, built of wood, was plain except that at varying intervals in a horizontal direction, a wave pattern rippled across it in relief. The quiet beige of the walls was matched by a carpet and ceiling of the same color. Its high key gave a sense of gayety and life. In front of this the values of any other color stood out vividly but harmoniously. The six large windows became a compelling unit to every passerby. . . . Only abstract mannequins of my own design were used, . . . and a mannequin who did not display the merchandise to better advantage than it could be displayed without her was regarded as a detriment. Under no circumstances was she allowed to focus attention on herself. . . ."

Here, then, was streamlining at work along one of the world's busiest streets. Bel Geddes also built a series of "window units," abstract shapes covered with various materials in different colors, which he systematically combined in the window settings depending on the color, materials, and predominant lines of the merchandise. Bel Geddes' method did not gain acceptance outside his own department, probably because display cannot be done so methodically without soon becoming dull, at least when in less capable hands than Norman Bel Geddes'.

In light of American displaymen's interest in European moderne, Bel Geddes' claim to have introduced abstraction into American display through his Franklin-Simon windows seems exaggerated. But his account of why he left theatrical stage design work for industrial design is telling of an attitude that seems to have been shared by many displaymen and other designers of Bel Geddes' generation. Automobiles, trains, ships, and factories were all to Bel Geddes "more akin to life" than theater because they represented a fusion of science and art that improved the daily lives of great numbers of people. Bel Geddes, who designed theaters among a vast number of other projects, by no means rejected theater as such. But drama for him was not limited to the actions that take place on the stage. Display and architecture were for him projects with inherent drama. The main development in American display, by the midthirties, is that it became highly theatrical.

The Art Deco movement interested American businessmen from at least two points of view. One was aesthetic, according to various trade papers, including *Women's Wear Daily,* which observed that Art Deco represented perhaps the first successful attempt at applying machine-age production methods to the making of finely crafted goods. The Metropolitan Museum of Art in New York provided study resources for businessmen, including lectures on current design trends and various consulting services, while it promoted modern American design work through various museum displays. Businessmen were also attracted to the Art Deco movement because it furnished prototypes of merchandise that could be sold with a relatively new approach to marketing: promotion of the style rather than the utility of the product. There was nothing new in 1927 about yearly changes in styles of fashionable hats and dresses, but Deco designers began applying similar considerations of styling to toasters, bookends, radios—both to useful and luxury items. The distinction between the two types of merchandise was itself brought into question, both by the aesthetic of moderne and by the more subjective appeal of the new type of advertising.

As Deco furniture and other artifacts were imported for sale in American stores and with the appearance of the Art Deco style in American magazine and newspaper graphics, in architectural ornament, and in other facets of design, American displaymen realized that the sales effectiveness of window display in a rapidly changing machine- and graphics-oriented society would depend on its ability to remain current in overall design as well as in fashion. A dramatic acceptance of the Art Deco style occurred in the windows of many American stores in late 1927 and 1928, beginning in New York with Macy's, Stern's, Wanamaker's, and Saks Fifth Avenue. Deco windows were also seen in Oakland and San Francisco, Boston, and St. Louis. Arthur V. Fraser at Chicago's Marshall Field adapted a "Fraseresque" version of moderne. The style was also tried in small cities. *Display World* reported from Iowa in 1928 that "when Davenporters passed down the streets to view the glories of the season's attire in the shop windows, they were having an opportunity equal to that of shoppers in the larger cities of the country. As to the details of the window displays, it was found that futuristic motifs characterized them. . . . Elaborate styles and fabrics were in evidence and all the charming paraphernalia of spring helped to make the windows spectacular." One American displayman who had only reluctantly yielded to the trend instructed colleagues: "Three elements should predominate in the 'modern art' [i.e., moderne], display, namely: color, form, and what is hardest of all to get, a feeling of movement."

Artificial flowers, which had been far and away the favorite display prop twenty years earlier, did not entirely vanish from major American store windows in 1927. But wherever the Art Deco style was adopted, traditional florals with their poignant or more often quaint romantic connotations were for the time being shelved.

The Art Deco interest in turning hard and unusual materials into aesthetically pleasing objects of machine-perfect finish was interpreted by American window displaymen through the use of a hard-edge line in background graphics and through the invention of display props and mannequins whose predictable shapes and material make-up had been fabulously transformed. For example, *Display World* reported that in a display at Saks Fifth Avenue, "a tulle evening frock was draped on a modernistic figure resembling a violin. Fans, gloves and other accessories were placed on an equally bizarre table. Another figure was shaped like a leaf, and a third expressed the swagger of a modern flapper." Commenting on his Christmas windows for 1935 at Filene's, Winthrop B. Frye remarked that "the long-accepted red and green for Christmas decorations had been supplanted by modern chrome. The effect was most exhilarating. . . ." Glass fruit, bronze and wrought-iron decorative screens, formica surfaces, metallic papers, and chrome display stands were among the fixtures, props, and materials imported or copied from France.

The leading French manufacturer of Art Deco mannequins, V. N. Siégel, wrote that "the old wax mannequins were too realistic to respond to the abstract form assumed by architecture and decoration. . . . The elegance of the modern woman had to be emphasized and her slenderness brought into relief." Papier-mâché mannequins such as Siégel's were also much lighter weight and less easily broken than wax ones and were easier to modify as to color and form. They were also heat-resisting unlike wax, "withstanding successfully," one advertisement grandiosely stated, "the penetrating rays of the powerful window lighting used in the modern store." Siégel's mannequins, the manufacturer insisted, were to be viewed only as fixtures, as abstract elements of the overall architecture of the window and store. In 1928, Siégel opened a remarkable new showroom in Paris for which the building facade had been done in polished aluminum and glass. This was among the very first building fronts to be so constructed, and it was considered, as *Display World* remarked, in keeping with Siégel's reputation for advanced design. Less than two years earlier, the trade journal, in giving its first notice of Siégel's work, had described his Deco mannequins as "grotesque." In the meantime, hundreds of the figures had appeared in windows all around the U.S. And in 1928, one American manufacturer already had his own "new indestructible mannequins moderne" on the market.

Some American department stores not only showed their affinity for moderne in their windows, but also presented Art Deco exhibitions of their own. Halle Brothers in Cleveland was the first store to do so, with its Art in Industry Show in 1927. The following year, Macy's held its second annual International Exposition of Art in Industry close on the heels of Lord & Taylor's Exposition of Modern French Art. At Macy's, products of France, Germany, Austria, Italy, Sweden, and the United States were shown, including glassware, rugs, ceramics, jewelry, fabrics, silverware, metalwork, and furniture. The Metropolitan Museum of Art took part in planning the Macy's exhibition. Lee Simonson, who was known for his design work for the Theatre Guild in New York, planned the interiors for the show, making use of various metals, asbestos, cork, and other raw building materials as elements of decor. "They have a beauty of their own," Simonson remarked, expressing a view that at the time was unorthodox among designers, "and they also eliminate much of the labor that is necessary for the finishing of woods." Simonson argued that if the benefits of modern design were to be enjoyed by a large segment of the population, such less costly materials would have to be accepted for interior design. Deco window display, he said, was all too often practiced in a lavish style, and could not be taken by interior designers as a source of inspiration.

THE THIRTIES

American displaymen had in fact been experimenting during the twenties with inexpensive materials such as crepe paper, cork for decorative surfacing, corrugated metal for Deco background effects, and so on. During the early thirties, their experiments continued, but with unaccustomed urgency. The Stock Market Crash of 1929 and the Depression had a devastating effect on most display budget allotments and on morale at many stores. Many displaymen lost their jobs as business and trade slowed down and many stores went out of business. *Display World* published position-wanted ads each month. In January 1931, the magazine reported with uncharacteristic bluntness that New York's holiday windows "lacked imagination. . . . If ever a jaded and discouraged New York public needed an exhibition of optimistic ingenuity it was the beginning of this year." The journal added somewhat melodramatically that "gumption" was more vital than "vision": "Don't consider yourself an artist."

Attention in the trade magazine shifted from New York and Chicago to developments in smaller cities around the country. During the Depression the major city stores maintained extravagant levels of display that smaller stores increasingly could not afford to copy. At many stores, including many found in the cities, "moderne" was exchanged for "modern"—a more matter-of-fact and often drabber approach, with a reliance on relatively plain display letterings as the main graphic element and with inexpensive materials such as crepe paper stressed, sometimes ingeniously.

Activity on the part of regional displaymen's associations around the country increased. The New York Metropolitan Display Men's Club held it first annual convention in 1930, and Pacific Coast, Central Illinois, and Down-In-Dixie groups held similar meetings that year.

The Depression had the effect of imposing a discipline on displaymen in the way that they used and reused materials. They became more familiar with the many resources that had first come on the market five or ten years earlier. One New York fixture company, for instance, found an economical way of converting papier-mâché mannequins into far more costly metal ones. Felt, although already in use for many years in some stores' windows, was praised now as the "ideal fabric for today's background," for its "ease of handling, fresh brightness, durability, and comparatively low cost." Textured paints, it was found, could be used as an "economical and effective medium for working up three-dimensional finishes." Photo cut-outs provided another inexpensive means of attracting passersby, and *Display World* recommended their use to its readers.

Display World continued to report on European display trends, offering the poster-clear manner of German and Swedish window display as a model of work that not only cost little to produce, but also stated a sales message with unusual economy of expression. "The continental displayman," it was observed, a little one-sidedly perhaps, "permits nothing to interfere with the presentation. Where decorative background effects in a hosiery display are introduced, they consist of hosiery cut-outs or hosiery trademarks; where figures are used it is done in such a way that they become a vital part of the composition rather than mere decorations, as is often the case in American displays of hosiery."

Surrealism and Display. Display, then, as Norman Bel Geddes and others had already pointed out, was a medium with resources that were not only ornamental but symbolic. When the American economy showed signs of recovery around 1936, and displaymen had more money to spend on their windows, this understanding of the store windows was applied in some of the more memorable windows that have been designed: the surrealist displays of the late thirties and forties.

The question of fantasy led some surrealist artists to become involved in window display. Salvador Dali, Marcel Vertès, Tanguy, and the surrealists' friend Cocteau, among others, saw in the store window a ready-made daydream—a commercial one to be sure, but then what surrealists rejected were certain values, not the products, of the marketplace. (The surrealist Man Ray worked as a fashion photographer.) Dali and Marcel Vertès were among those to design jewelry or fashion and fashion illustrations as well as window displays at this time, and they did so with an understanding that clothing and jewelry, the human body's adornments, are never far from mask and costume and as such may be properly seen within fantasy's realm.

In surrealism, displaymen found an effective device for getting people to stop at their windows. On a busy city street, a bizarre window drama had a better chance of attracting a rushing passerby into momentary attention than did a fastidious rendition of a drawing room. While surrealist painters in their more serious works often tried to sabotage a viewer's expectations by composing an image that called for contradictory responses of laughter and tears, displaymen were more restricted in the extent to which they could shock their audience. Intent as they necessarily were on encouraging an impulse to buy on the part of window-shoppers, they did not want to induce a state of terror in the process. In surrealist displays, the bizarre and the macabre were usually treated in terms of parody or romance. Thus Dali and other artists may have found in window display a chance for self-parody.

Surrealist display implied, with the harlequin's dumb refusal to be taken quite seriously, that the world was not to be taken quite seriously. Life, as the designer Schiaparelli, with whom Dali sometimes collaborated, said, is "a-*musing*." Life occasionally seemed to furnish evidence to this effect: "Flood-relief workers in an inundated section of Pittsburgh, Pennsylvania, were horrified," *Display World* reported in April 1936, "when the catastrophe was at its worst, to see the body of a woman floating down one of the submerged streets. A score of them splashed through the water to the rescue. The body was lifted from the stream, and it was not until that moment that they realized that the figure was not a flood victim but a mannequin which had drifted from a show window."

In a surrealist work of art, an image of familiar objects disturbingly transformed—a melting watch, a grand piano being dragged across a room by a man in harness—might be calculated to unlock secret springs of the unconscious. In a window display for Saks Fifth Avenue, by contrast, Marcel Vertès placed a mannequin patient on an analyst's couch above which an unconscious wish—concerning a new dress the store was featuring—had materialized. The frivolousness of the wish was offered as its own defense. A surrealist window, then, was surrealism at play, but such a window as Vertès' might be obliquely satirical, nonetheless, while also going about the business of selling fashion.

As to the seriousness with which surrealist windows were taken by the public, store managements mainly wanted to know whether passersby would be induced by the displays to go into their stores. The question for management had little to do with surrealism as such, but with the publicity value of window display as a "free show." The question was answered almost from the first, when in 1936, the first Dali windows were installed at Bonwit Teller in New York, and considerable publicity resulted for the store as well as for the artist.

It was Dali's second series of windows, however, done in 1939 for Bonwit Teller, that are especially memorable. In the interim, displaymen around the country experimented both with what became known as "modified surrealism" (surrealism in which the bizarre tended towards the beautiful rather than the grotesque) and with other, nonsurrealist types of "free show" display, with by far the most astonishing of the latter appearing at Lord & Taylor for Christmas, 1937.

The battery of five Lord & Taylor windows, designed by display director Dana O'Clare and Henry F. Callahan, who was then O'Clare's assistant, contained no merchandise at all, but instead showed a miniature winter landscape with large Christmas bells swinging slowly above while outside the muted sound of distant bells came from a concealed amplifier. The store, by its own reports, received nearly half a million "comments, letters and telegrams" in praise of the windows. Originally scheduled to run for five days, they remained for a month with full-page newspaper ads announcing the unprecedented holdover. The windows cost only $2,000 to construct and install, and were repeated the following year; in addition, they were shown for the Easter of 1938 at the Galeries Lafayette in Paris. *Display World*, commenting on what from its standpoint was the unexpected success of no-merchandise windows, generalized that it must be "the idea in the display and the way it is handled that counts."

The mood expressed in the bell displays could probably not have been less jaded or less like the mood shown in the 1930 Christmas windows seen around New York. The bell windows probably symbolized for much of their large audience relief that the worst of the Depression had apparently passed. The displays were related to Christmas without being especially Christmasy, festive rather than religious in treatment, and their popularity established the store's tradition of doing holiday windows of this kind.

In New York at this time, Jim Buckley and Tom Lee produced remarkable windows that were often surrealist in treatment, but without being derivative of Dali. Buckley, who became the leading exponent of the idea that display can be an independent art, showed that apparently strange but calculated reorderings of objects, abstract elements, materials, and symbols might put into sudden sharp focus certain qualities of the merchandise on display. To bring out the seasonal lightness of a group of dresses, for instance, Buckley displayed them on mannequins of fantastic cast, made entirely of chicken wire and birch bark, in a series of displays called "Elegantes in Birches."

Tom Lee was among the first displaymen to use a complete window bank as a single stage, and there was always an element of surprise at least bordering on the surreal about what would be seen in them. Skiers in chair lifts, a large cool drink on the sand in a beach scene (see page

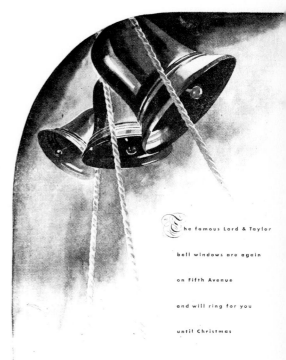

The famous Lord & Taylor

bell windows are again

on Fifth Avenue

and will ring for you

until Christmas

A full-page ad in The New York Times *announced the return installation of Lord & Taylor's Christmas windows, first shown in New York in 1937. The bell windows were repeated each year until 1941. Courtesy Lord & Taylor.*

Compare the surrealist display figure by Tom Lee, designed for Bonwit Teller in New York in the early 1940s, with the mannequin dressed in pearls by Salvador Dali (page 109). Also compare it with the deadpan treatment of a mannequin by André Breton and Marcel Duchamp (page 37). Courtesy Sarah Tomerlin Lee.

105), a forest in which the tree trunks had built-in shelves for perfumes and cosmetics (see page 108) were among his window designs.

Lee, who was Bonwit Teller's display director in 1939, helped Salvador Dali install the latter's windows of that year—a pair of displays that Dali named, "Midnight Green" and "Narcissus White." No fashion was shown in either display.

The "green" of the first window represented envy. A female mannequin was posed langorously in bed, wrapped in a blackish sheet. The headpost of the bed was a large, horned bison head. In the background, a male figure set in the pose of "The Thinker" was just visible in shadow. Gray cobwebs hung down like a shroud in the rear of the window.

In "Narcissus White," the main prop was an old-fashioned claw-footed bathtub completely covered on the outside with Persian lamb. In the tub, dozens of detached white mannequin hands reached upward, each holding up a hand mirror that was tilted to catch the reflection of the figure seen about to enter the tub. The mannequin chosen for this window was also an old-fashioned type, with the pristine china-doll face of the kind seen in windows around the country in 1900. The figure had blond hair down to her waist that was, however, overrun with beetles and bugs. Tears of blood had formed on her otherwise idyllic face. The mannequin was dressed only in a mantle of white coq feathers. The walls were covered with quilted satin in hot pink and were studded with mirrors.

The store management found the windows too suggestive and made certain changes that apparently so displeased Dali that he reentered the windows to make repairs. In the process, the bathtub somehow (probably by accident) was pushed through the window glass and onto the sidewalk. Dali grandly stepped out after it and was promptly arrested. The chronology, according to the trade paper *Retailing*, was as follows: "The display was finished Thursday morning at nine, it was in until noon, at one it was revised, Dali came along at five, he and the bathtub came through at five-thirty, the curtain came down on the windows for good at six, during the night new displays were installed." Among Dali's defenders was the local plumbers' union, which called the store asking for a photograph of the windows that had so glorified the bathtub and their profession. But no picture had been taken as there had not been time.

The Dali windows of 1939 provided a shrewd commentary on the psychology of display. "Midnight Green" made it clear that display is usually a form (if occasionally also an art) of seduction. A window display was always a tug at the impulsive side of a passerby's nature. But with refinements in display drama and graphics, windows were becoming more articulate and so very possibly also more persuasive. "Narcissus White" pointed to the likelihood that passersby looking in a store window often momentarily forget they are not looking in a mirror. The appeal of material possessions, as Dali luxuriating in the fact implied, is often an appeal to vanity. Narcissus, in the legend, plunges to his death in pursuit of his reflection. But, then, the history of fashion and of the decorative arts generally suggests that given the choice, people rarely base their decisions about their clothing and at least some of their other possessions on necessity's requirements alone.

Desire for the "good life" is, of course, the very tendency that advertising since the twenties had increasingly exploited in campaigns designed around a product's style. And it has been plausibly argued that following the Depression, the so-called American Dream, which was founded on the assumption of unlimited plenty, had been so badly shaken for most people around the country that advertisers found it increasingly necessary to devise other, more ephemeral substitute-dreams with which to put across their client's products. And as a result, advertising turned more to fantasy for its sales appeal from then on.

After the Depression, window display in general did become more theatrical. The best work in display was done for fashion, fashion accessories, and objects of fine design, which were themselves products of fantasy of an aesthetically high order.

When surrealist display was not attempted, the trend was towards "theme" displays, in which the window might be related to a current event, the season, or some idea suggested by the styling of the merchandise—a plaid dress might be shown with beefeater hats and

Tom Lee designed this theme display for Bonwit Teller in New York in 1939. Entitled "Slide Rule Exclusives," the window decor is based on a fabric pattern. Photograph by Worsinger. Courtesy Bonwit Teller.

bagpipes. In displays of this kind, displaymen could not, as previously, rely mainly on a knowledge of tasteful room decor and other stock trims in presenting the store's merchandise week after week. A greater familiarity with materials was required to make the relatively unusual images presented in the displays cohere in visual terms. Many kinds of knowledge were often for the first time applied in designing a window: a knowledge of dance, opera, literature, and theater, of exotic decors and costuming, of trends in contemporary art, of decorative handcrafts of all kinds. In 1929 the artist Archipenko had designed a series of sculptured background panels for Saks Fifth Avenue in New York. In Portland, Oregon, display director Malcolm Tennent became well known for his monumental abstract settings for fashion at Meier & Frank Company. Some displaymen merely used works of art to lend prestige to merchandise in a window, but others were able to relate a piece of fine art to the other objects on display in a way that showed insight about the design of all the elements in the window.

In everyday life, as the surrealists demonstrated, objects of all kinds are already charged with our fantasies. As displaymen drew more on these fantasies as part of their materials, the results they achieved from an aesthetic standpoint depended more than previously on the quality of imagination shown in the finished design. Not all fantasies, displaymen found, are equally beautiful or dramatically engaging. Talented displaymen showed that a store's goods can be sold by presenting them on terms that are aesthetically neither timid nor obvious. As display became more a medium of fantasy, its potential expanded not only for banality and overassertive bad taste, but also for a high degree of expressiveness and wit as applied art.

To supply the needs of theatrically oriented display departments, large studios formed during the thirties to supply props and fixtures that often had direct bearing on the merchandise. For instance, large silk flowers might be used not only as ornament but also as a way of pointing up the delicacy of a dress fabric. Dogs made of chicken wire and covered over with leaves might become seasonal symbols and light touches of dramatic stage-setting. When Arthur V. Fraser at Marshall Field decided to restage the fashion displays of the 1937 Paris Exposition in his windows, he took his detailed sketches to Silvestri, a Chicago display studio. When papier-mâché reindeer for a Christmas window were needed, displaymen from around the country might place their order with Staples-Smith in New York. At the bigger stores, a larger percentage of propping and fixturing was built in-house, and the display studios served a supplementary role while providing smaller stores around the country with window decorations that they were not equipped to make themselves.

The studios employed a variety of artists and craftsmen, including perhaps a trained theater designer, an interior decorator, an advertising layout man, each of whom was a capable sketch artist, as well as carpenters, metal workers, painters, workers in composition and coach metalwork. By drawing on such diverse specialties, the studios opened up many new sources of ideas for display.

Mannequins. A related development in the midthirties was the design and production of the first fashion mannequins that were both rela-

tively lifelike in appearance and practical for use in a display window. The wax figures that were available around 1910, many of which were imported from Germany, had melted in the windows as display lighting became more powerful and more directed. Many such figures were really tailor's dress forms with a pair of arms and head attached afterwards; the figures stood on a pedestal, which was concealed by the extremely low hemlines of most women's dresses before 1926.

Other mannequins had originally been designed for waxwork exhibitions that were a popular form of entertainment during much of the nineteenth century. In Charles Dickens' *The Old Curiosity Shop*, the little heroine, Nell, is forced to lodge in a room where a troupe of wax figures are kept. For Nell, their very perfection becomes an image of an inner deformity: "They looked so like living creatures, and yet so unlike in their grim stillness and silence, that she had a kind of terror of them for their own sakes, and would often lie watching their dusky figures until she was obliged to rise and light a candle, or go and sit at the open window and feel a companionship in the bright stars."

Most early wax mannequins were not considered tastefully done and were not widely used at stores. Better figures, both female and male, were available around 1912. The males, mainly character types, also melted under the lights and like the females, weighed 200 pounds or more and usually broke if tipped over.

Mannequins were first made of papier-mâché in the Art Deco style around 1925 in France. But they were mainly exercises in Deco styling rather than attempts at lifelike models of a woman or man, and they went out of style in a few years. They were revived during the early fifties and again during the early seventies.

Also around 1925, an American, Cora Scovil, devised an offbeat solution to the problem of how to display beautiful clothes without getting involved in what amounted to a wax museum operation. Scovil's "patch posters" were large, tapestried fashion illustrations, with the

Cynthia (center) and designer Lester Gaba (left) are interviewed by Robert L. Ripley on the "Believe It or Not" radio show in 1939. Two years earlier Cynthia had appeared on the cover of Life *magazine and again in 1937 as the central figure of a "Life* Goes to a Party" *pictorial feature. Courtesy Lester Gaba.*

figures in each poster drawn to scale. A displayman, taking a dress, a pair of gloves, or a necktie he wanted to show, could pin it into place on an appropriate figure in the poster, which was then hung in the window. The patch-poster idea borrowed ingeniously from the proven technique of using magazine covers or printed posters for display. The clothes on a Scovil poster could be rapidly changed, a fact that some displaymen may have played on for the fun of it, keeping regular passersby on the lookout for sudden changes of detail. The versatile posters could also be used for interior display, and were extremely popular for many years.

During the thirties, Cora Scovil also designed the first fashion mannequins to be termed "glamorous," including a series modeled after leading Hollywood actresses. Hollywood promoted its stars as ideal types of beauty, as "film goddesses" who apparently paid a lot of attention to their clothes, lent their names to advertising, took part in fashion promotions, were seen dressed in a certain way in the national picture magazines, and so on. It thus made great sense to base mannequin designs on the stars. Scovil's Greta Garbos, Joan Crawfords, and Joan Bennetts had plaster bodies and stuffed cloth arms, legs, and heads, with long felt eyelashes and felt lips, all done with a theatrical lightness of touch that made them all the more glamorous. They were, however, hard to pose and proved to be too difficult to work with.

Cora Scovil's assistant at this time was Mary Brosnan, who became the leading mannequin designer in the early forties. Scovil's chief rival was Lester Gaba. In 1934, Gaba introduced his celebrated "Gaba Girls." Almost to the extent that Charles Dana Gibson's magazine illustrations of the Gibson Girls had popularized an image of the modern American woman of the 1900s, Gaba's figures represented a thirties type of beauty and worldliness in display windows all around the country. Unlike the abstract Deco figures, both Scovil's and Gaba's mannequins had *personality*. The Gaba Girls, modeled after young New York socialites, were said to have "bold glances" as well as snub noses and heavily rouged lips. In 1936, Gaba produced "Cynthia," whose popularity he played to the hilt by appearing with "her" at the Stork Club, in parades, at parties, and perhaps most appropriately on the radio version of "Ripley's Believe It or Not."

The publicity stunt may well be the American equivalent of the Dadaist put-on, characteristically modified by its commercial intent. P. T. Barnum had been a master of this type of flamboyant display. Barnum's famous remark that "There's a sucker born every minute" expresses an idea at least partly shared by the Dadaist Marcel Duchamp when he declared a blue shovel and a toilet to be works of art.

In 1939, the suburban development of Levittown made headlines when the first completed house was cut out from a giant cellophane bag in which it had been wrapped. Between 1963 and 1968, the artist Christo wrapped many objects, including store windows, although for very different ends. Duchamp himself designed at least one window display in New York during the midforties at the Gotham Book Mart, with the collaboration of André Breton. In the window of that store, which is known for its support of experimental writing, Duchamp

The reflection of André Breton is at the center of this Breton/Duchamp collaboration at The Gotham Book Mart in New York after publication of Breton's Arcane 17 *in 1944. Inclusion of the poster (left) with the semiabstract nude by Matta nearly resulted in the arrest of the shop's proprietor, Miss Frances Steloff, who covered the offending parts with a morals squad officer's calling card and the word "CENSORED." The headless mannequin reader with the spigot leg was entitled "Lazy Hardware" by the artists. Photograph by Maya Deren. Courtesy Maya Deren Collection, Boston University Libraries.*

placed a headless mannequin dressed as a chambermaid with a little apron and a book in her hands; she was apparently reading—except for the fact that she had no head.

Thirties mannequin designers in general tried to give their figures more grace and more of an appearance of movement and activity than previously. Duchamp's window was, among other things, probably a humorous commentary on such attempts. The old wax display figures, especially those of women, had stood almost as stiffly as cigar store Indians, giving the impression of a passive, stay-at-home type of existence, which, around 1910, was still considered to be the most respectable of feminine pursuits. During the thirties, by contrast, a series of women's sportswear mannequins by Lillian Greneker were featured at Lord & Taylor—a golfer, tennis player, and diver. They were considered remarkable for the accuracy of the modeling and the poses and reflected changing social attitudes, which the public display of the figures did not initiate, but helped to popularize.

In France during the thirties, V. N. Siégel, the principal designer of Art Deco mannequins, introduced an unusual group of figures that were freehand wire outline sculptures—three-dimensional doodles elegantly drawn. They had great class, and although clothes did not fit as well on them as on the more full-bodied conventional mannequins, they provided novel relief from the more realistic figures that, if not done extremely well and handled with the right dramatic distance, were always on the verge of becoming grotesque parodies of the types of beauty they were meant to suggest or illustrate.

As display mannequins were increasingly modeled and typed after debutantes and film stars, mannequins at times also were seen in movies. The surrealist Luis Buñuel, in his 1955 film "The Criminal Life of Archibaldo de la Cruz," took the mannequin-as-ideal-beauty to its grotesque limit, showing the burning of such a figure, which, in the context of the story, represents an unattainable woman whom the male character chose to pursue in the first place because of her resemblance to the mannequin. The plot is further complicated by the fact that the man's intention for the living woman was not love at all, but murder. In the end, the two of them are seen walking away happily together, an ending that has been variously interpreted as an absurd surrealist gesture and as an eleventh-hour commercialization of an otherwise deeply disturbing scenario. More recently, in Fellini's "Cassanova" (1977) and in Truffaut's "The Man Who Loved Women" (1977), mannequins also appear as symbols of a man's inability to love a woman.

By contrast, in "Shall We Dance?," a minor Fred Astaire–Ginger Rogers film of 1937, Astaire goes for a spin around the dance floor with a department store mannequin, and the chorus line at one time appears as mannequins all wearing life-size Ginger Rogers masks. Every girl, the story suggests, aspires to be that mannequin of mannequins, the star. Here again is the myth of the dream-girl, treated, perhaps, with Hollywood's usual lack of inquiring intelligence, but also, at least, with a grain of salt.

For the 1937 Paris Exposition, V. N. Siégel designed perhaps the strangest and closest to fine sculpture of the mannequins of this period. The figures were 7 feet tall, made of plaster in a bisque color, with featureless heads. Each fashion designer represented at the exposition was given a troupe of the Siégel figures on which to show his or her new dress designs. Because the mannequins were so large, special clothes had to be made. Lanvin posed her huge models on a gigantic horse and lion. Schiaparelli disliked the mannequins so much that rather than dress one, she lay an unclothed figure down across her assigned exhibition space, covered the body with fresh flowers, and put up a clothes line along which she hung her new collection. Siégel's mannequins were afterwards tried at various stores in the United States, where, however, their careers were short-lived. One Chicago paper described the figures as "truly modern in the sense that they create emotion without going into detail." Siégel himself commented that what might be characterized as "the somewhat disturbing emotional effect" of the mannequins corresponded to a "feeling of youth and rhythm and movement toward a new life."

Siégel's heroic optimism, like the attitude expressed in 1938 and 1939 at three major expositions in New York City, San Francisco, and Glasgow, Scotland, looked forward to a thoughtfully designed urban world of the future. Most efforts in this direction were soon interrupted by the outbreak of World War II.

Among the first "action" mannequins (figures shown doing something other than just standing around) were Lester Gaba's "kandid kamera kids," shown in this Marshall Field window of 1940 designed by display director Arthur Fraser. Photographer Marian Stephenson originated the "candid camera" style of photojournalism during the 1930s. This was possibly also the origin of the phrase "candid camera," which Gaba applied to these display figures. Courtesy Lester Gaba.

Contrary to what one might expect, World War II did not force a serious curtailment of creative activity in display. During the Depression, many displaymen had learned to make do with scarce or low-cost materials. Similar measures were taken during the 1940s. Ads for paper sculpture props first appeared about 1942 in *Display World*. There was no shortage of fresh flowers for window decor, and displaymen wanting to give passersby a cheerful sight during that often gloomy period frequently did so with flowers. Antiques and decorative fabrics were as always available, and in general, displaymen during the war became more conscious of the city in which they worked as an informal collection of display resources — museums, antique shops, and other neighboring stores — which they might call on for an occasional borrowed prop in return for a credit line. The more inventive display manufacturers also continued to do well during the war. In 1942, Cecilia Staples, president of one such concern, actually doubled her firm's work space, where props and entire window settings were designed and made in papier-mâché and other nonpriority materials.

At least since 1900, display windows had at times been used by merchants to convey a patriotic or public service message to anyone who happened to be passing their stores. Fourth of July, Washington's Birthday, and Christmas windows were familiar sights all around the country, and in some, though by no means all, of these displays, no direct attempt was made to sell merchandise, although such windows did, of course, attract attention to the particular store. Early in 1942, *Display World* urged that "there is no better way of upholding citizen morale than by producing window and interior displays that give a lift to the spirit. Displaymen and retailers must realize that just as long as retailing continues, so must display."

Bond drive, victory garden, and other propaganda displays with a war theme proliferated; 300,000 such windows appeared nationally in July 1942, and remarkably, there were 1 million displays of this kind only one month later. Marshall Field gave over a room on its ninth floor to serve as a "Victory Center," with photo exhibits and other news of the war.

Photo blow-ups were often used in windows in the form of cut-out figures and scenery that were combined with three-dimensional props for uncanny illusions of spatial depth and journalistic realism. "Realism," *Display World* observed, "counts a lot in victory displays." Background murals done in an heroic style like that seen at the 1939 New York World's Fair were also used in many windows.

A series of mannequins were placed on the market, which glorified the "business girl," who in many cases took over the work of men who had entered the service. "Pat, Jean, and Helen will spark sales," an ad in *Display World* asserted.

Many more women found jobs in display departments during the war than previously. But as in many other types of business, women seem to have been regarded by management as temporary replacements for displaymen away for the war. When the war was over, the number of women working in display departments declined, returning almost to the low level of that before the war.

Many women were, however, involved in display through related

WORLD WAR II

Throughout World War II, Lord & Taylor's vice president and later president, Dorothy Shaver, used a corner window with the glass removed as a platform from which to urge people to purchase war bonds and to support the war effort. Courtesy Lord & Taylor.

jobs. Dorothy Shaver, as vice president and then president of Lord & Taylor during the forties, took an extremely active role in the store's display and other promotional efforts. Dorothy Hood was Lord & Taylor's fashion advertising designer. Mary Brosnan and Lillian Greneker were leading mannequin designers. D. G. ("Dot") Williams was the most prominent mannequin manufacturer. Mary Brosnan designed for Williams' company for many years. Cecilia Staples was president of a major display house, Staples-Smith. Virginia Roehl was a New York display photographer and writer.

Just as important to the morale-raising effort were window displays that apparently had nothing to do with the war. At Bonwit Teller, for instance, Tom Lee designed a series of windows in which scenes from classic children's tales were shown. When Dana O'Clare, display director at Lord & Taylor, went into the army, Henry F. Callahan took charge, designing the first of his many gala theatrical windows, mainly at the time, on a shoestring.

In June 1942, Tom Lee entered the Army Air Corps and was assigned to the intelligence division and to work on the design of camouflage. Norman Bel Geddes also had a leading part in the development of camouflage, which is, in effect, a wartime application of various techniques of graphic art. In 1942, The Museum of Modern Art presented a circulating exhibition, "Camouflage for Civil Defense."

That same year, in a development that looked towards the war's end, the display trade journal started a new column, "The Play World," reviewing theater and ballet set and costume design, museum shows and restaurant decor, all as related subjects of professional interest to display personnel.

THE STATUS OF THE DISPLAYMAN

"The displayman has the greatest opportunity to gain his due recognition in the department store structure if," Albert Bliss, a leading display manufacturer urged in 1939, "he will study the principles of fluorescent lighting."

Fluorescent lighting had first been introduced to the public at the 1939 New York World's Fair, which was, in effect, a grand scale demonstration of the modern (as opposed to moderne) vision of the future, as conceived by industrial designers Norman Bel Geddes, Raymond Loewy, Walter Teague, and others. Improved lighting and air conditioning were among the modern features that many merchants installed in their stores following the Depression, forcing their competitors to do the same. Even merchants who had maintained highly exclusive clienteles found that to stay in business they needed to attract a wider audience of potential customers, and so modernized. As stores were made more convenient for shoppers, the display staffs came to be regarded by management as in-house experts on the large variety of techniques, fixtures, materials, and machinery needed for store modernization.

Fluorescent lighting, as Albert Bliss noted, could increase foot candles, reduce watt consumption, lower the operating cost of air conditioning, and eliminate dirt from ceilings. It also showed the true color of merchandise more accurately than yellow incandescent light and so might substantially reduce the number of color returns and exchanges. Lucite first became available for fixturing during the late thirties, as did heavy-duty display papers such as Traton, Velton, and Flexton with their world-of-the-future names so typical of the generation of designers that also produced the Empire State Building, Rockefeller Center, and the 1939 World's Fair. Dramatic colored lighting was also featured at the 1939 Fair, illustrating that modern industrial design, if stripped of cumbersome ornamentation, might nonetheless have drama. And although this type of lighting had been introduced for display several years earlier by Helen Cole at Bonwit Teller, it became widely accepted for window display after 1939.

The displayman's position within the store also improved as management became more aware of the sales effectiveness of well-designed windows. Often in the past, shopkeepers and managers had merely put up with display and would probably rather have closed down the windows and extended the selling floor to eliminate what they saw as a waste of space. But during the midthirties, marketing surveys, including several by stores, were conducted in an effort to find what types of advertising were most effective. The management of The Emporium in San Francisco, for example, conducted this experiment: "We charge our department managers," one of the store's vice presidents wrote in *Display World*, "a daily rental for any window which their merchandise occupies. We offered fifty buyers their choice of a window which rents for $30 a day and an ad in our best newspaper medium, which would cost $30. Eighty-eight per cent preferred the window." At Marshall Field, the display department itself charged rent for the merchandise shown in its windows. At Saks Fifth Avenue under Sidney Ring, buyers had to compete on a first-come, first-served basis to have their clothes displayed. The managements of some large chain stores were also becoming more display conscious.

Display and National Magazines. During the midthirties, national magazines, which ten years earlier had influenced display only indirectly by setting standards of graphic modernness and excellence, recognized display as a related medium with which it was worth coordinating their advertising. In 1936, *Life* magazine set up an entire merchandising department "to help the retailer take advantage of this new magazine which had direct value to him." The *Life* operation had several parts. A group of traveling representatives toured the country to advise retailers on how best to use *Life* tie-ins in their window and counter displays. In retailer's trade papers, *Life* ran ads reporting on the success of such tie-in campaigns and gave lists of merchandise soon to be advertised in *Life*. The magazine sent reprints of these ads by direct mail to retail executives around the country. *Life* also furnished for display purposes cover blow-ups, advertised-in-*Life* posters, stickers, arrows, tent cards and counter cards, *Life* Modern Living posters, and so on. Lee W. Court, Filene's display director at the time, commented that "that red and white *Life* card is about as arresting a device as I know. Our tests show that it invariably gives our displays extra stopping power. The reason is plain, I think: it associates what we are showing with the most interesting and exciting magazine there is . . . *Life.*" Probably, in the smaller cities and towns, which became less and less their own economic and cultural centers during the thirties, the sales value derived from the nationally popular photo weekly would have been even greater. Other magazines provided similar services to retailers, most notably *Vogue,* among the fashion magazines.

For the first time, magazine ads also pointed to display as an advertising medium of authority. A 1936 ad in *Fortune* for no-glare printing papers, for instance, compared this development in paper finishes to invisible glass, a relatively new type of glass that eliminated blinding daylight reflections on a display window. No-glare paper is to the magazine reader, the ad suggested, as invisible glass is to the window-shopper. Ten years earlier, such an ad would not have been considered as especially convincing within business circles.

Industry Developments. The International Association of Display Men continued to meet each year, but disputes among regional factions led to its weakening and eventual break-up during the late forties. At the 1942 gathering, a new group, The National Association of Display Industries, formed with twenty of the largest display manufacturers as its charter members. This organization remains today as the oldest and largest display group, sponsoring biannual trade shows in New York, giving annual display awards, coordinating advertising, and providing a number of other services. During the sixties, a major regional group, The Western Association of Visual Merchandisers, formed, providing similar services for a membership centered around California. Displaymen themselves have not had a national organization since the IADM. The demise of the IADM reflected the fact that as the more unusual types of display work were increasingly found in a few of the larger cities, the display manufacturers in those cities saw their interests as more distinct from those of the various regional organizations.

Conditions imposed on American retailing by the nation's involvement in World War II also led to greater responsibility for displaymen. Because the war took many people away from their usual jobs at stores, managers began to experiment more with techniques of self-service retailing. Merchandise display in this type of arrangement became a substitute for personal salesmanship. This development in turn further encouraged management to consider display in terms of an overall effect, a "store image" of which the windows were a part. A store image as presented in the windows could serve as a short-hand message to passersby as to types and styles of merchandise the store specialized in. In cases where several stores offered more or less the same things for sale, the store image provided a more subjective appeal to customers. Stores, like the products sold inside them, were increasingly being seen and redesigned in terms of style.

In 1944, the display manufacturer Albert Bliss coined the term "visual merchandising" to refer to this more comprehensive and more systematic approach to merchandise presentation. John E. Mertes, chairman of the department of marketing at the University of Oklahoma, suggested in 1949 that the "visual merchandiser" was to be concerned with the activities of store design; planning; store and departmental identification; customer traffic control; store layout;

space-sales analysis; fixturing; window, interior, and counter display; merchandise signing; outside exhibits; and display research.

The transition from display to visual merchandising (the latter term did not gain wide currency until the early seventies) did not necessarily imply an end to window theater (or to what one manufacturer referred to as the "nuttiness" of display), or, more generally, to the interest in treating merchandise display as an applied art. Around 1950, for example, the first American boutiques were designed as experiments in interior display at various department stores. The concept had been adopted from France. Just before the war, Schiaparelli opened a little shop in the downstairs salon of her headquarters on the Place Vendôme. The shop-within-a-shop apparently caused so much excitement that other designers soon opened their own, planning the tiny selling floor around a theatrical centerpiece—a golden chariot, in one case; an exquisite birdcage, in another—from which the boutique also took its name. Among American stores, Bloomingdale's in New York adapted this idea with the most inventiveness and alacrity. By the sixties, some large stores had begun to look more and more like world's fair exhibitions or design museums in which all the objects on display were for sale.

1949. Two events of 1949 served as measures of the state or progress of display as an industry and as an applied art. The Museum of Modern Art as part of its twentieth anniversary celebration held an exhibition, "Modern Art in Your Life." The purpose of the show, according to the catalog, was to illustrate how "the appearance and shape of countless objects of everyday environment are related to, or derived from, modern painting and sculpture" and to show that "modern art is an intrinsic part of modern living." Concerning window display, the catalog's authors, Robert Goldwater and René d'Harnoncourt, said, "The sudden shock of surrealism's dream world is wonderfully suited to the show window" as well as to "the stage set and the more ephemeral sort of advertisement." In this way, the museum gave its first recognition to that form of modern decorative and commercial art, fine examples of which were then on view not far from its door as well as in many other cities.

New York University's School of Retailing made a study in 1949 of the effectiveness of window and interior store display. This was by far the most systematic inquiry made to that time. The surveyors attempted to find a way of measuring display "readership" that would be more or less comparable with the circulation figures of magazines and with radio and television ratings. By counting and classifying passersby at selected store windows that had been specially dressed with merchandise not advertised in any other medium and then by comparing the statistics with figures for the same windows under normal circumstances, certain fairly consistent findings were obtained: about 91 percent of the men and 92 percent of the women who passed the windows had been either casual "lookers" or more attentive "readers"; the lowest average performance for a display delivered a readership of 25 percent of the men and 65 percent of the women; virtually every customer who, when interviewed inside the store, said he or she had seen the displays but had not stopped to read them attentively, could nevertheless identify the displays in photos and often could also supply various details, such as colors, to the surveyor. The surveyors also learned, to their disappointment, that most stores did not keep accurate records correlating display of merchandise with sales. Their findings suggested unmistakably, though, that the correlation, if determined, would be relatively high.

1950s DISPLAY

After World War II, American window display entered a period of romantic celebration and considerable fun. Hat displays by Gene Moore at Bonwit Teller faithfully illustrated such distinctly mad captions as "Oh, for Two Heads!" and "Nothing Like a New Hat to Give You a Lift!" At Lord & Taylor, Henry F. Callahan staged elaborate theater scenes—a series of cave windows done entirely with coal was one from 1949—as well as windows based on the show in the theater lobby and on the society lives of "the most fabulous people in the world." The fashion photographer and stage designer Cecil Beaton wrote of New York at this time that "the window-dressing is one of the city's chief features. The displays at Lord & Taylor's or Bonwit Teller's have brought about a style of presentation that utilizes surrealist and neo-romantic effects with great taste and creates peepshows which are almost works of art in themselves. Each fashion lives brilliantly, but dies a weekly death as it gives way to the next display."

The "Phantom," an invisible mannequin, first startled passersby at Hattie Carnegie, a New York specialty shop, sometime during the midfifties. Clothes and accessories were wired into a natural standing pose, but the mannequin itself was omitted or replaced by separate photographs of matching arms, face, and legs. The Phantom idea was whimsical, perhaps, but very sophisticated. (It had also been tried in 1937 at Harrod's in London.) It shared with "Miss Live Wire," a dancerly mannequin made entirely of steel wire mesh, an attitude of lightness about materials, which in turn lent a quality of fantasia to

Lord & Taylor display by Henry F. Callahan in New York in 1954 illustrates Callahan's "theater of social occasion." Mannequins are based on fashion drawings by Dorothy Hood used in the store's newspaper advertising (see illustration on opposite page). Photograph by Malan Studio, Inc., New York. Courtesy Henry F. Callahan.

display. "Glamorous" and "fabulous" were the words that seemed for the people who led or followed or were otherwise caught up in display and fashion to best describe the style and atmosphere of the late forties and fifties.

The Phantom and Miss Live Wire were novelty figures. The fifties mannequins of the more solid, dependable type had a more sensuous cast than had been achieved previously. The use of plastics made it possible for the first time to have the designer's delicate modeling retained in the finished form, which was also more durable than the figures of wax, plaster, or papier-mâché.

In New York, Mary Brosnan was the leading designer of mannequins, selling to stores all around the country and to Europe. Lillian Greneker was her chief competition. It became more common during the fifties for a display director at a store that could afford custom-made mannequins to take part in the actual design work. Gene Moore at Bonwit Teller, for instance, did a figure modeled on the actress Vivien Leigh. Mannequins were also designed after fashion models and other figures in the fashion world. Poses and settings in which various displaymen placed mannequins in their windows also influenced the fifties style of fashion and commercial photography. Display manufacturer Cecilia Staples, who for many years had done her wire and papier-mâché sculptures mainly for use in window display, received more orders during the fifties for figures that were to be photographed in the round for print advertising.

Social Commentary on Display. That the best American display work with its extremely high level of taste had some influence on other forms of advertising was a benefit to advertising as well as perhaps to the many people exposed to its messages. As Cecil Beaton, along with virtually every other observer of midcentury American society, noted, "America is primarily a country of advertisements." Beaton in his

Fashion sketches by Dorothy Hood were a feature of the store's newspaper advertising, shown here from 1951. Courtesy Lord & Taylor.

Cecilia Staples' New York studio, Staples-Smith, designed and manufactured papier-mâché Christmas fantasy settings and figures for stores around the country, such as this one for Carson Pirie Scott in Chicago in 1951. Staples also made the Delman rabbit (page 82 and elsewhere). Photograph by Idaka. Courtesy Carson Pirie Scott.

Portrait of New York of 1948 considers display to be a thing apart from most other types of advertising, which, by contrast, he views with what seems like curious skepticism mixed with the relieved detachment of the traveler who is only passing through: "Advertisements fill the radio programmes with their clamorous exhortations. Doctors give testimonials for cigarette advertisements; movie stars attest to the fact that they use a certain face soap, mascara or deodorizer. Book matches, bearing the names of shops, hotels and restaurants, accumulate so that the activities of the past week can be traced to create a sort of match diary. . . . Even the sky is used as a medium of advertisement. . . ."

However, not all social critics and observers have distinguished between display and advertising in general, as Beaton does. Percival and Paul Goodman, for instance, in their classic analysis of modern American urban society of 1947, *Communitas*, see display as a typical feature of an economic system in which growth of production largely depends on artificial demands created by advertising. As production has since the 1920s become more and more a means to the end of consumption, work for most people, they argue, has become less satisfying for its own sake and is instead viewed mainly as a necessary evil to be tolerated in return for consumer rewards. The great cities, in the Goodmans' understanding, have especially since the 1920s represented the centers of interest for such consumer rewards as well as the places of amplest supply: "The heart of the city of expanding effective demand is the department store. . . . Here all things are available according to desire—and are on display in order to suggest the desire. The streets are corridors of the department store; for the work of the people must not be quarantined from its cultural meaning."

To the extent that the Goodmans' analysis is accurate, it adequately accounts for a quality of ennui and personal dissatisfaction that probably almost anyone living in contemporary urban society will recognize and almost certainly will at times have experienced. If their study is lacking in any way, it is in their failure to allow enough for an immense variety and eccentricity of individual human response to the city which in itself is so complex and often contradictory a phenomenon.

An opposite view from the Goodmans', expressed by the architect Marcel Breuer, seems equally plausible: "The first question we ought to ask ourselves in talking about the city is why we want to preserve it at all. The answer is all around us: the city serves an important human need. It has the drama of the market place, it has the excitement of personal contact, of infinite possibilities. It has the intensity of speed, it is a constant demonstration of vitality."

It may well be that many of the same aspects of urban life, display among them, that cause feelings, as the Goodmans suggest, of ennui at certain moments of the day become sources, as Breuer suggests, of delight and positive energy for the same individual or for others at other moments. The experience of city living is profoundly an experience of getting and spending, monetarily, emotionally, physically, spiritually.

Cecil Beaton, curiously enough, sketches the particular kind of intensity of New York around 1948 largely in terms of notes about windows. New York, Beaton reports, has relatively little of what he calls "window life": "In Italy, Portugal and Spain a large part of the day is spent leaning on the window-sill," but in New York, by contrast, most people seem to be in too much of a hurry. While "the English hide at their meals as if eating were something immoral," Beaton finds that "in broad daylight in a shop window, the American shamelessly eats" his or her lunch over a counter. In the Automat, Beaton observes the New York preferences for speed with efficiency and for gregarious window display ingeniously combined: "The Automat has a clinical cleanliness—the tables are washed continuously, even the slots through which the nickels pass are polished many times a day. Around the marble walls are rows of dishes, each an appetizing still-life framed in chromium. Apple-pie rests in one brilliantly lit frame, in the next a rich slice of raisin cake is the *objet de vitrine*, in another a sandwich, neatly wrapped in opalescent paper." In the weekly changes of the city's major window displays, Beaton sees an image for what he found to be a common attitude among New Yorkers toward their worldly belongings. The observation might be applied equally to the Goodmans' and to Marcel Breuer's description of the city. "They hold no sentimental feeling for their possessions," Beaton says of New Yorkers. "There are few old attic collections in New York."

Gump's. Displays of a romantic, often very elaborate kind were seen during the late forties and fifties at stores in Chicago, Los Angeles, Boston, Dallas, St. Louis, and Philadelphia, among other cities. Most of the unusual display work was being done for fashion.

But at Gump's in San Francisco, a style of display that was unlike any work seen in the United States until that time was evolved by the store's owner and displaymen Don Smith and Herb Renaud. Gump's

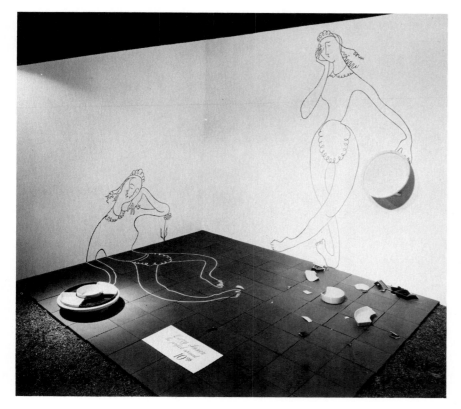

Elegant mannequin doodles by display director Herb Renaud of 1951 illustrate the simplicity achieved in early windows at Gump's in San Francisco. Photograph by Skelton Studios. Courtesy Gump's.

had concentrated not primarily in fashion, but in products of excellent design, gifts, and fine art works, with most of the store's merchandise imported from the Far East. The intention in developing a Gump's style of display was to relate the windows to aesthetic principles shown in the merchandise.

The early Gump's windows had much variety. Sometimes surrealist theater elements appeared in them; other times the windows became abstract in a way that resembled Mondrian's sense of space. What characterized the Gump's style in all its variations and what made it similar in nature to Oriental design was an insistence on simplicity of composition; a respect for the raw, unfinished qualities of materials; a preference for lightweight, inexpensive decorative materials (for instance, plywood rather than mahogany panelled walls); and an interest in taking seriously from the standpoint of design a wide variety of types of objects, a much greater assortment of things than had previously been displayed with artistry at an American store.

Television and Display. During the fifties, fashion magazines and popular magazines such as *Life* continued to offer the best possibilities for free fashion publicity, just as television does now, and it was common practice for magazine covers to be shown in window display for a tie-in effect or as a courtesy, as they had been since the 1930s.

"'Tomorrow,'" *Display World* had predicted in December 1939, "we may see style shows and fashion presentations televised into every home and accepted nonchalantly as part of the regular television program. Even advertisements in the form of dramatized displays are not far-fetched. The part the displayman will play in such arrangements lies in the future. . . ." By the midfifties, television and display had begun to influence each other in a variety of ways.

Television designers had at first turned to commercial theater and film for analogous techniques of staging and propping. But both these media operated on large budgets supported by the relatively long runs of the shows. By contrast, television, like display, involved a great deal of rapid turnover. By the early fifties, many former displaymen were finding jobs in television studios, and television stations around the country subscribed to *Display World* as a source of technical information and lists of suppliers.

Displaymen with experience in card writing had the skill needed to

Magazine covers are part of window graphics in this early 1950s display by H. McKim Glazebrook at I. Miller Shoes in New York. Photograph by Malan Studio, Inc., New York. Courtesy I. Miller Shoes.

design TV titles and station identification slides. Displaymen knew where in a given city to find fabrics, seamless papers, lighting fixtures, foliage, plaster, paints, photo blow-ups, papier-mâché work, metallics, and screen-processed art, all of which were needed for television production. Display lighting technicians could readily adapt to television lighting work. Displaymen with a knowledge of carpentry could design and build permanent sets such as kitchens for cooking shows and the office and parlor settings that were for a long time used for interview programs. Display personnel were often also seen as desirable candidates for television management positions because in addition to their other skills, they were used to working on strict weekly schedules, also necessary in television.

Television and to a larger extent film and photojournalism also influenced window-shoppers and window-shopping. The technical quality of these media tended to make display audiences more critical of a store's style of visual presentation, especially when attempts were made in windows at illusions of realism. And as color television, film, and photography became more commonplace during the sixties, the standard of comparison for display became all the more exacting. Occasionally, displaymen used closed-circuit television or video screens as part of a display—a technique like that used fifty years earlier when advertising posters were used in windows to add the impact of a more widely circulated type of image to the window display.

While television commercials may not be said to have made window display less effective as a selling medium—no matter how much the characters in them may resemble dummies—the immense popularity of television in general from the late forties on, almost certainly made window-shopping less important to millions of people as a form of entertainment. Television to a large extent preempted the free show that the store windows had provided at least from the time of the Dali windows on. As people watched more television, they went out less in the evening merely to stroll and window-shop.

The post-war movement to the suburbs also contributed to a decline in the custom of strolling and window-shopping that, as recently as the midfifties, had led to gathering of hundreds of people, complete with police barracades, along the window banks of the New York stores known for the best displays. This kind of interest, by contrast, is now shown only at Christmas time at a few of the city's stores.

Shopping centers and more recently shopping malls at first had few or no display windows. Display has always been directed mainly at pedestrians, and these shopping areas were designed more to attract shoppers arriving by car. As many of the larger city stores became part of bigger corporate organizations that had much of their capital invested in windowless suburban stores, budgets for display in the cities became more closely regulated in relation to fluctuations in the economy. Displaymen, or rather visual merchandisers as they were increasingly called in this corporate atmosphere, had charge at many stores of interior as well as window display, in some cases with responsibility for both urban and suburban branch stores all around the country. It also became more common for a store's director of visual merchandising and planning to become a corporate vice-president.

THE SIXTIES
AND THE
SEVENTIES

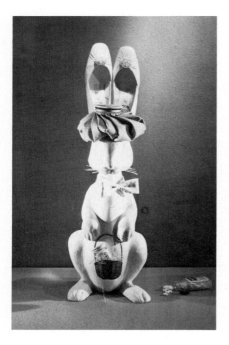

Display director Howard Nevelow's Delman rabbit becomes "Harvey" in 1970. Photograph by Malan Studio, Inc., New York. Courtesy Delman Shoe Salon.

Compared with display during the fifties, just as much thoroughly remarkable work was done during the following ten or so years, but sixties display was more the expression of individual talents than of an overall attitude or style that could be traced through other facets of popular culture or developments in the fine arts. Society was too divided over questions of basic values for display, which is an expression of the less serious, man-does-not-live-by-bread-alone side of life, to have had the momentum of a widely shared style. The war in Vietnam, the movement for black civil rights, the rise of youth culture, changing attitudes towards sexuality, and the reemergence of a women's movement were all developments that display as a commercial medium was not on the whole equipped to deal with. During the early 1960s, when black mannequins first appeared in the windows of a few stores, for instance, this was a recognition of social gains already fought for and won, although, it must be added, that John Quinn at Bergdorf Goodman and other displaymen who followed his lead in integrating their troupes of display figures did so at the risk of losing some of their stores' older customers.

Lighthearted and graphically sophisticated Pop Art effects were seen in some store windows. Andy Warhol, Jasper Johns, and Robert Rauschenberg all worked for Gene Moore at Bonwit Teller, starting in the early fifties. Once a year, through the early 1960s, Moore showed the serious work of artists on his staff in window displays that were in effect the first major public exhibitions of Pop Art. In general, Pop Art was itself too close to commercial art to do for display what surrealism had done in the late thirties.

Nevertheless, some of the most beautiful and original work in window display appeared at certain stores around the country during the 1960s, especially in New York and San Francisco. Gene Moore, who had become display director at Tiffany in 1955 (from 1955 to 1962 he designed Bonwit Teller's windows as well as Tiffany's), continued to work on the miniature scale of the store's shadowboxes to create settings of enchantment in which wooden spools and hat pins, crystal and diamonds have become each other's ornament in unexpected turns of dramatic grace and graphic imagination. At Saks Fifth Avenue, Henry F. Callahan, who became display director there in 1956, greatly enhanced the store's reputation for elegance and fashion. His windows were always done with impeccable taste and expressed a high degree of sophistication, as in the "Phantom" windows and through various uses of dramatic lighting and controlled but extravagant detail. For the Christmas of 1965, Callahan decorated the entire main building facade as a giant pipe organ. His influence was seen in Saks stores all around the country.

During the early sixties, Howard Nevelow at Delman in New York did the first of his very elegant and often slightly daffy displays of shoes. Dan Arje, Robert Benzio, William Mac Elree, and Gene McCabe are among the designers working with fashion who made various experiments in display, often adapting a graphic approach. McCabe, for instance, worked at stores that had not previously been known for unusual windows; he introduced Mylar and neon as display materials (see page 164). At Gump's in San Francisco, Robert Ma-

Soft
and
easy...

This is the way to
drift through Summer.

Young Colony, sixth floor

Top 17⁰⁰
Skirt 21⁰⁰

Top 23⁰⁰
Skirt 21⁰⁰

honey became display director in 1963, further simplifying the remarkable windows at that store.

Various developments were made in display resources. Many new plastics became available for fixturing and decorative purposes. "Cultured" marble, made from polyester resins, proved a good substitute for classical stone. Acrylic paints were first used for resurfacing during the sixties.

Adel Rootstein introduced a line of fashion mannequins whose realism had a harder edge than Mary Brosnan's figures and was strangely photographic. Occasionally, as display again became theatrical during the early seventies, actresses held fashion poses on the street in front of a window with Rootstein mannequins, teasing passersby into staring or watching with entertained looks (reactions to these surrealist gestures were tellingly varied) as people might stare at the scene of an accident or watch with delight a performance of street theater.

Early in the seventies, at about the time that blue jeans passed from being a sign of rebelliousness into fashion, a noticeable change oc-

The fans here have a Pop Art connotation as well as a more abstract sculptural presence in this ready-to-wear display by Robert Benzio at B. Altman & Co. in New York in 1971. Photograph by Malan Studio, Inc., New York. Courtesy Robert Benzio.

Midseventies minimal style of ready-to-wear display is shown here at Henri Bendel, Inc., in New York in 1977, designed by display director Robert F. Ruffino and designer Phillip Smith. The rear wall opens directly into the store. Compare this with the trompe l'oeil illusion created by Tom Lee in 1938 (page 108). Photograph by Jerry P. Melmed. Courtesy Jerry P. Melmed.

curred in the windows of certain New York stores. The Pop realism of "situation windows"—in which passersby might see a baby being born, a murder in progress, or pairs of unoccupied shoes arranged in action poses—marked a return to theatrical display. The best windows of this "theater of the street" had a deadpan wit and rude awakening approach to sexuality that could be satirical or poignant. Occasionally, a designer was able to take advantage of the publicly exposed, explicitly commercial setting of a display window as part of the dramatic material of a situation. The surprise quality of the propping in these windows—real objects as opposed to display manufacturers' props were preferred, for instance, telephone booths, cigarette butts, nuns' habits, and policemen's night sticks—added to their fascination as a theater of mock realism, which, even in still life, could at times have greater visual immediacy than television.

As a result of the situation windows, people became aware of display as a phenomenon as they had not been for more than twenty years. The style was tried at many stores around the country, but most of the imitations tended toward sensationalism, the limits of which, as far as most store managements were concerned, were soon exhausted.

During the midseventies, display became more simplified, with a clean-cut, graphic approach to fashion display. An effort was made, perhaps more than ever previously, to have the clothes stand on their own with only a light and sometimes apparently only an improvised style of propping. These often more austere, "architectural" windows reflected an economic situation in which most store managements and most shoppers were carefully watching their budgets and avoiding unnecessary frills. The windows also suited a preference for simplicity shown in the design of the clothes.

At least a few trends concerning the future of window display could be detected by the late seventies. A surprising development was the appearance of itinerant displaymen in different parts of the country, who periodically changed various windows in relatively small cities

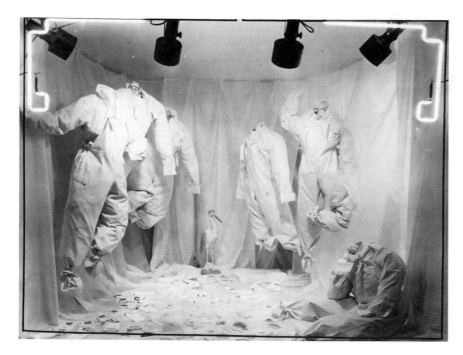

Judy Simonson created this clothing shop display for Reminiscence in New York in 1978. Photograph by Fifth Ave. Display Photographers, New York.

and towns where mass-produced displays had been the rule for many years. In major cities, more small shops showed an interest in display, largely because of an increasing need to compete with department stores that had incorporated many small shops within their own walls. More types of stores experimented with attractive display: record and book stores, antique and gift stores, toy stores, florists and bakeries, design stores, less expensive jewelry stores, stores selling inexpensive "antique" clothes. More attention was given to the display of men's clothes, both at large and small stores. At some shopping malls, many of which had originally been designed with no display windows, a few windows were installed at the entranceways to attract attention to current features within the mall. In city neighborhoods where efforts were made at economic revival, more care was shown in merchants' shop windows; this was both an expression of neighborhood pride and an aid in redevelopment, since the windows attracted the business of passersby from both in and out of the neighborhood. By contrast, in neighborhoods and cities of increasing poverty and related social problems, little or no attempt was made at display. In Detroit, for instance, it became necessary to board up the windows of many stores. From this standpoint, enclosed shopping malls were seen by wary developers and their insurance companies as not only more "convenient, environment-controlled shopping facilities," as promotional advertisements were apt to style them, but also as better security risks than were the stores facing public streets.

In 1974, the display trade magazine again changed its name, from *Display World* to *Visual Merchandising*, as recognition of the fact that the people who designed windows were increasingly involved in many other aspects of their stores' operations, often including management itself. The growth of several once relatively small cities, with the dispersion of talent that this implies, suggested that window display practiced at a level of artistry might start to appear, as it had not for thirty or more years, in many places around the country. This mainly depended on decisions about city planning that had yet to be made by the late seventies. A trend toward creating more outdoor pedestrian malls, for instance, would probably lead to more interest in window display; a preference for suburban-style enclosed malls would produce the opposite result.

The two main styles of seventies display formed a kind of coda or summary in miniature of the medium's expressive resources— dramatic and graphic or architectural—as they have developed over more than fifty years. Ideas in display tend to be repeated. The handling of an idea is what gives a window its originality. Display always involves an address between individuals in which the handling of the idea becomes an expression of the designer's individuality; the aesthetic integrity of the work is a show of respect for the passerby who has been momentarily diverted by the window. Display at times serves as what one designer has called "a bridge from the seriousness of museums to the paper and string of everyday life." This is the sense in which window display, carried out within the terms provided by a particular store, is an applied art.

Each time designer Gene Moore changes the window in the Madison Avenue Bookshop, the "man" there is recast in a different role (shown here in 1978). Photograph by Fifth Ave. Display Photographers, New York.

PROFILES

ARTHUR V. FRASER

On opening its new main store in 1907, Marshall Field & Company announced an unprecedented display policy. The store's windows were to be made as beautiful as possible with expense a "secondary consideration." Field's display director was Arthur V. Fraser. At a time when most window displays consisted of dreary parlor scenes or stocky assortments of merchandise, Fraser did windows in an epic style that drew on classical sources of decor and on a highly refined sense of design and composition. He was among the first displaymen to realize the value, when showing fine merchandise, of putting relatively little of it in a window. And although, as Fraser was well aware, his displays made the merchandise in the windows look very expensive (as in fact it usually was), his windows drew large audiences of passersby. As *The Merchants Record* observed: "People do not look in Field's windows for bargains—they look in them for STYLE!"

In 1922, when archeologists unsealed Tutankhamen's burial tomb, Fraser saw a brilliant possibility open to him. Fraser's regular displays, many of which were based on Egyptian decor, would have appealed to passersby who admired pomp and a grand show. The windows had a quality of spectacle, but with exquisite taste and style, such as had made dioramas (of "The Great Fire of London" and so on) popular sideshow entertainments during much of the nineteenth century, and had perhaps also given rise to the claptrap grandiosity of the Chicago Exposition of 1893.

For Marshall Field's very wealthy customers, Fraser's windows may well have resembled the decor of their own homes and apartments or reflected their interests as collectors or travelers. But the discovery of the Egyptian tomb was a news event that attracted widespread public curiosity and interest. When Fraser restaged the treasure rooms across the entire span of Marshall Field's sixty-seven windows, the displays, which were perhaps the first to take advantage of a timely theme on such a scale, became the talk of Chicago.

When, however, in 1927, the moderne or Art Deco style of display gained wide acceptance at American stores, Fraser merely adapted certain Deco elements to his own style of "massive effects" and classical harmonies. Deco artists and designers had themselves drawn on Egyptian and other ancient non-Western design sources for ideas. And Fraser, who must have been an accomplished art historian, was able to treat the moderne style not merely as a form of newness, but in terms of its origins. "Aside from the distinct modern note in line, design, color and mannequins," *Display World* reported of a series of windows of 1929, "there is much in the other elements of the decorative treatment that is as distinctly 'Fraseresque' as can be. The Egyptian influence, the specially designed furniture, fabric-covered walls, posing of figures, use of columns and general neatness of detail—all are earmarks of Fraser's work that would be immediately recognized by the average person. . . . The great corner window at State and Washington has a flat covered background of corded moire in sand shade. In the center of the background a half-arch doorway with three steps leading down to the window floor is covered with dark taupe carpet. At the right of the arch and at the end of the steps a huge single column extends from the floor to the ceiling. Egyptian figures, done in modernistic manner in tones of light gold, tan, light and dark sand, ornament the column. Flanking the steps on the left is a tall pedestal bearing a modernistic deer finished in light gold. Four figures, decidedly modern in feature and finish, display gowns. The furniture in all of the windows is likewise 'art moderne à la Fraser.'"

The ceremony with which window display was associated at many stores around the country is suggested in *Display World*'s account of Marshall Field's fall opening windows for 1927. Once or twice a year as recently as the late thirties, many stores mounted special opening displays that corresponded, for the stores of the larger cities, to the seasonal openings of the European fashion designers and that in rural areas, took on various associations with the planting and harvesting of crops. (This custom was never adopted in New York, apparently because it was not considered sophisticated to go through the fanfare.) In anticipation of the event, the stores' windows would be closed down completely for perhaps a week. In 1927, Field's seventy-fifth anniversary, the store's windows were curtained twice that long, which, together with pre-opening newspaper advertising, worked up "considerable interest thereabouts," it was reported. On the Saturday before the opening, ads in the local papers announced that the curtains would rise on Monday at 10:30 A.M.: "Long before the appointed time crowds waited the unveiling, and promptly at the stroke of half-past ten all the curtains began to rise at the same time. The interest was intense, and during the entire day and until late at night there were literally thousands of people milling around the block, studying, observing, admiring, and exclaiming over the beauty of these wonderful displays." The main bank all along State Street was in the Egyptian style "rich in colorings of blue, greens, purples, gold and black."

In 1937, Fraser and his assistant, L. Sternetzhe, visited the Paris Exposition, where they met with the mannequin designer V. N. Siégel and arranged for a set of his bizarre seven-foot-tall creations to be shipped to Chicago. Fraser made detailed drawings of the Chirico-esque walls and scenic decorations featured at the Pavilion de l'Élégance and reproduced three in identical pale blue and pink plaster in Field's windows. Silvestri, one of the major display houses at the time, made the settings which, one Chicago paper predicted, would "first shock, then electrify" viewers.

The giant Siégel figures, for which special clothes had to be made, were hard to work with, and they were not seen for long in Field's windows or elsewhere around the country where they were tried. Although Fraser retired in 1944, the exposition windows were in a way his swan-song—as monumental as had been the Egyptian treasure room windows of 1922, but full circle from them in their extreme modernity. A Worcester, Massachusetts, displayman had observed in 1928 that "the modern man and woman finds little time for the elaborate and mystical." But these qualities were the real pillars of Fraser's work, the chief mystical claim of which supported what *Fortune* magazine in 1936 called "the Midwestern faith that 'Field's has everything.'"

Arthur Fraser's treatment of color was considered a part of the signature of his windows, and although the surviving photographs of

Arthur V. Fraser display in Egyptian style. Marshall Field & Co., Chicago, 1925. Courtesy Marshall Field & Co.

his work are black and white, at least a few of these can be matched with *The Merchants Record* descriptions: "The back and side walls were flat, covered with black broadcloth or similar material. The floors were carpeted with dark blue carpet. The columns under the arch were finished in gold from the top down to where the carved ornamental work stops and from this point down to the base the finish is of a dark but distinct blue. The ornamental base upon which the figures are posed, which, it may be noticed, constitutes an important part of the decorative scheme, consists of a solid piece of black lacquer about eight feet long and between nine and twelve inches high. The dragon figures at each front corner of this sub-base, are finished in gold rubbed over with green. The top surface upon which the figures are posed is finished in mottled blue effect."

In October 1936, *Fortune* characterized Fraser's windows, not altogether fairly, as "stately and dull," an assessment more or less shared by screen director Vincente Minnelli, who worked briefly in Fraser's department and who recalls the experience in his memoirs. Minelli adds, however, that he learned from Fraser a sense of professionalism and a meticulous care for detail that carried over into his own theatrical career. *Fortune* in its article went on to observe with apparent admiration that at Marshall Field the "section [department] managers must buy window space as they would advertising space from display director A. V. Fraser," who was almost certainly the first displayman to gain the authority of a store executive.

Sidney Ring, Saks Fifth Avenue's first display director, was best known not for his window design work, but for his business acumen as part of the store's management and for a variety of innovations in display technique that he made and that other designers later developed in their windows. Ring worked at Saks for more than thirty years, from its opening in 1924 to 1956.

In his work Ring was always very interested in finding possible relationships between display and the arts. In 1927, for instance, Saks' windows were among the first in the country to be designed in the Art Deco style. Ring hung draperies of silver gray in semioval arrangements along the rear walls for a Deco ripple-shadow graphic effect. The folds of the material were drawn taut, rising toward the ceiling in V-formation. As a frame around the windows, Ring placed broad satin bands, three to a side just behind the glass. The satin ribbons were hung from the top down and cut at the ends at parallel angles to create a lightning zigzag Deco proscenium.

The Art Deco window settings were, however, used by Ring in only six of the store's thirty-one display windows, while traditional windows were continued with mahogany paneling and room settings elsewhere along the store's facade. This was perhaps Ring's controlled business sense in action, a cautious experiment that gave the store's less adventurous customers plenty to look at if Art Deco did not happen to be their cup of tea. Yet, Ring seems to have aimed at startling passersby when the six Deco windows were first installed, and it was remarked somewhat quizzically by various observers that some of the abstract metal mannequins shown in the windows resembled musical instruments, one with large pegs for a head and a body curved in the shape of a violin.

As display director, Ring was always a methodical businessman. He insisted that all thirty-one windows, most of which were changed once a week, be handled with similar attention. "There are no side windows at Saks," he declared. Following each window installation, Ring prepared a complete list of all merchandise in the windows, with full details on colors, prices, and window locations. Copies were distributed to every store department and posted there as an aid to store personnel in answering shoppers' questions. Ring also kept a detailed inventory of all display fixtures and properties on the premises, with a special list of those items it would be costly to replace.

He secured working conditions for himself and his staff of sixteen that were described by *Display World* in 1947 as a "display director's dream": "Space is not allotted to each buyer, but goes on a first-come, first-served basis. The buyers request space and receive it until all is reserved. This policy forces them to state their requirements well in advance of the time their merchandise is to be featured," leaving Ring and his assistants time to make their extensive plans with deliberation.

Staff meetings were held before preliminary sketches for a set of windows were done and again just after. The sketches were then refined and props built. All but the most complicated props were designed at the store and then contracted out to various display houses. At another staff meeting, color schemes were debated. Then at a meeting also attended by the buyers specific items were selected for each window.

SIDNEY RING

The final meeting was held after the actual installation. "This meeting," *Display World* reported, "is a gloomy one when the effect has somehow or other failed to hit the target dead center. And the bitter fact is that this reaction prevails more often than not; the department consists of a group of perfectionists. . . ."

Such planning probably left relatively little room for improvisation. Ring himself referred to his displays as "pictures" and as "still life" versions of a Broadway production. His aesthetically most successful displays tended to be those planned as abstract graphic designs rather than as the festive, stagey type of display that became very popular around New York during the late thirties.

Ring's interest in abstract art took many forms. He commissioned the Russian sculptor and painter Archipenko to design a continuous sweep of background panels for the store's windows. This was in 1929, and the work was done in long strips of blond wood arranged horizontally in a stepwise pattern. There were various curves and sculptured holes in the unbroken surface that made it quite beautiful. It was a sensation at first, and it remained in the windows unchanged for several years.

In 1937, Ring showed that collage, as a medium of visual play between two- and three-dimensional elements, is a likely source of inspiration for display. Ring admired a series of painted mural decorations by a German-American artist, Mme. Annot, and he invited her to work with him on a set of windows. In each display a large panel was placed upright with a cityscape or underwater scene sketched across it. Each panel was framed in such a way as to suggest to the passerby that it was really the bottom of a large gift box. Various small articles of merchandise were pinned to each panel, fitted in with the scene in the painting in a collage. A mannequin in each window appeared to be looking in these fantasy boxes filled with gifts.

Occasionally, Ring's ventures into theatrical display were great successes. Perhaps the best of these was a series he had designed by Marcel Vertès, an artist known for his paintings as well as for fashion illustrations, cover designs for *Vogue,* and for the beautiful, atmospheric watercolor illustrations that he did for Schiaparelli perfume advertisements. Vertès' windows, designed in 1945, were surrealist dream sequences with cloud backgrounds. In one window, the setting was a phantom room in which the moldings were there but not the rest of the walls. This was Vertès' analyst window, in which a psychoanalytic patient's innermost thought was shown to be a Saks Fifth Avenue dress.

Ring was also partly responsible for bringing about one of the most publicized phenomena of thirties display, the advent of Lester Gaba's celebrated mannequin, Cynthia. It was Ring who commissioned Gaba to design the figure for the store and who brought the designer to meet the model Cynthia Wells, whose name was soon to become attached to the figure. Ring had wanted a mannequin that would represent a "typical Saks Fifth Avenue customer as she might look at the coronation of Edward VIII"—an upcoming event in 1936. Thus Ring was perceptive in surrounding himself with talent.

It was also mainly through commissioned work that Ring's windows

Rare display of whimsy by Sidney Ring.
Saks Fifth Avenue, New York, 1955.
Photograph by Malan Studio, Inc.,
New York. Courtesy Malan Studio, Inc.,
New York.

occasionally showed a sense of fun. At times, though, his own display work had touches of humor and whimsy. Once, for a display of hats, Ring made a series of scarecrow-like figures, each from a gray pole and wicker millinery head topped with a straw hat and with cherry blossom branches rising from the base of the figure. In one window, a pink serape filled out the form and was elaborately improvised from straw, pink millinery braid, fragments of chiffon and silks, pink flowers, and other scraps that might otherwise have been part of a hat. In front of the figure there was a low gray metal table with a glass top on which were displayed "pink porcelain" millinery in shantung, velvet, and straw, along with mother-of-pearl cosmetic accessories, pearls, and pink gloves. The window card, as in all Ring's displays, was an integral part of the composition. It pointed in this case from a hat on the table down to the ubiquitous carved wood scroll bearing the name of the store as a finishing touch. Ring, ever business-minded, wanted to be sure that window-shoppers would not forget the name of the store. The wood-carved signs remained in every window for more than thirty years as the signature that completes the picture.

TOM LEE

Evening window shoppers stroll past Tom Lee's "Trompe l'Oeil" windows. Bonwit Teller, New York, 1938. (For additional photographs of these displays, see page 108.) Photograph by Worsinger. Courtesy Bonwit Teller.

In the fall of 1938, the president of the University of Michigan, discussing his search for a new head coach for the varsity football team, told reporters: "Since the football team is the window display of the university, we might as well have a good one."

The remark is telling for us: Americans in the late thirties were conscious of display. They referred to it in conversation. Many thousands of people in cities around the country were aware of, and went out to see, window night when the new displays for the week were first opened. In New York City it was not unusual for 300 to 400 people to gather at one time around the windows of a major store. Display was a form of entertainment. It was theater. In New York, probably no displayman was more responsible for making the windows so popular an attraction at that time than Tom Lee.

"Amusing"—with all the comic and quasimystical associations of the word as Schiaparelli also used it—aptly described the world that Lee and his fellow displaymen recreated in their windows. Nothing inside a window was taken quite seriously. For a hat display, Lee might show a mannequin and a dog, with the dog wearing a woman's hat and the mannequin wearing a doggy headdress. Perfumes became "love potions" and were displayed in full-blown desert settings of exotic romance. Sheer stockings were turned into butterfly wings. Transparent plastic mannequins were lighted to glow from within, and odd little animals and dolls were placed on the window floor to give heightened scale to the mannequins by comparison. Surprise, as Lee noted, is always the key to display as a "free show"—a concept launched in 1936 with the Dali windows at Bonwit Teller. Timeliness, elegance, and romance were its main elements as Lee practiced it, along with an absurd, throw-away style of humor. But as with the whimsical but delicate little gloves that a woman of the late thirties was likely to wear—each glove fastidiously ornamented with one tiny petalled flower—the throw-away in Lee's highly theatrical displays was in the crazy idea, not the execution. Often Lee and his staff worked throughout the night to install the windows with impeccable detail.

Tom Lee was Bonwit Teller's display director when Salvador Dali designed his most memorable displays in the store's windows. Lee helped install the Dali displays and was in seclusion at a Turkish bath when Dali, having put a fur-covered bathtub through the window glass after his work was altered by the store's management, was arrested.

Before coming to New York, Lee had lived in Australia where he himself was known as a surrealist painter. Lee distinguished between surrealism in painting and in display when he called his "Trompe l'Oeil" series at Bonwit's "surrealist in treatment," because it was dedicated to romance rather than the macabre (see page 108).

The "Trompe l'Oeil" windows, among the theatrical display triumphs of the late thirties in New York, were based on an exhibit at the Julien Levy Gallery. Lee often made topical references in his windows to events in New York. This series involved various visual plays of forced perspective, creating for viewers, in one instance, the illusion of looking down from a treetop. In another window, the background was a colonnade that apparently receded far into the distance while a mannequin with a flying fish in her hair stood

One of a series of Tom Lee's 1938 "Trompe l'Oeil" windows, which tied in with an exhibition at the Julien Levy Gallery. Photograph by Virginia Roehl. Courtesy Sarah Tomerlin Lee.

languorously towards the front of the window. The windows had all been masked down to openings of about 5 by 3 feet, a decision considered especially daring since the merchandise consisted of costly furs, jewelry, and dresses by Chanel and Molyneux. Large display cards tied in the windows with the Julien Levy show. To further invite a comparison of the windows to art, Lee titled each display individually: "Wistful Vista," "Nest Eggs," and so on. For "Springing Up" and "Doors of Enchantment," he devised an unusual prop—trees with shelf drawers built into the trunks, all filled with luxurious dress accessories—the surprising magic and daft utility of which epitomized Lee's surrealist concerns as a displayman.

Crowds of passersby tilted their heads in response to a dream fantasy series inspired by "Sleeping," Schiaparelli's perfume for 1940, and by her "new" shade of aqua blue. Sayings from the "gypsy dream book" had been inscribed on various window cards. "A dream of falling," one caption warned pedestrians, "foretells misfortune." In that window, a mannequin was suspended head down from the ceiling—or dream-floor—onto which a console with stuffed satin ornaments and a satin padded chair had also been securely wired, all furthering the inverse illusion. A brilliantly lighted chandelier, painted in aqua, rose from the floor, which was padded with quilted aqua satin. A bottle of perfume was placed in the chandelier, with a spotlight trained on it to give the bottle the appearance of a lighted candlestick.

Lee's windows were noticed by Broadway producers, and in 1940 he designed the sets and costumes for "Louisiana Purchase," a Buddy De Sylva–Irving Berlin musical. Prior to the opening, various settings and props for the show turned up in Bonwit Teller's windows to publicize the event, giving the store's window-shoppers a preview.

Lee did a great variety of out-of-store consulting and design work, applying, in some cases, a display style of composition to other visual media. For a series of magazine ads for a fabric manufacturer, Lee draped lengths of each fabric over a chair and brought in graphically related props for balance—a stone lion for one setting—which he then photographed. During the late thirties, fashion photographers for the first time often found their inspiration in theme window displays such as those Lee specialized in—the use of, say, cigar store Indians and tobacco leaves as decorations for a display of dresses in "tobacco tones." Previously, the print media had always been the source of original ideas for displaymen to copy. But Lee and a few of his contemporaries raised window display to the level of an independent applied art.

Parades, balls, fashion shows, showrooms (including RCA's in Radio City), packaging and ad designs, office interiors, museum shows, hotel interiors were among Lee's other projects before and after World War II, during which he served in the Army Air Corps developing camouflage and working in Intelligence.

In 1947, Lee opened his own design firm, Tom Lee, Ltd., and at this time also decorated the windows and interiors of Bergdorf Goodman in New York. At Bergdorf Goodman, Lee's windows were simpler and usually quieter in tone than his Bonwit's displays, partly in keeping with the store's more restrained image at the time. But this was also because Lee thought that elaborately staged and accessorized windows were usually not appropriate for a specialty shop that did not have a large display budget and an extensive inventory. For a specialty shop, more emphasis is needed on the mannequin, less on the propping. For Bergdorf Goodman, Lee mainly chose props that blended into the background, like the decoration in a home. Working with the store's fashion coordinator in dressing the figures, he directed interest to the way that the clothes went together as an outfit or ensemble.

A funny series was done for Bergdorf Goodman with wallboard cut-out figures designed as dapper cartoon escorts for the mannequin in each window (see page 126). The cut-outs—one with six pairs of legs, another with a cuckoo-clock brain, and each with charms of its own—also brought out a merchandising point, since they provided a smooth textural foil for the rich brocade of the store's dresses.

Tom Lee's career was comparable in range to that of the leading industrial designers of his time, and it is probably because so much of his output was intact for only a week at a time that Lee's career as a whole has not been more generally remembered. Lee, who was an insatiable traveler, once surprised an audience by saying that Guatemala is as good a source of inspiration for display as France. It is surprising today to see in photographs of his work how contemporary the ideas of some of Lee's windows still are.

In December 1938, The Fifth Avenue Association in New York issued a dreary edict concerning window display along the "world-famous shopping thoroughfare." Motion in a store window would not be permitted as it might "cheapen" the avenue's atmosphere, so *Display World* reported. At this time live models were drawing crowds at the stores along Fourteenth Street, which thirty years earlier had been among the city's main shopping streets. The association's ruling came specifically in response to a series of displays done the previous month at Lord & Taylor by Dana O'Clare.

These were O'Clare's "blizzard windows," unveiled, as it happened, on an unseasonably warm day in mid-November. Coat sales immediately rose by 50 percent and remained at that level while the windows were on view. Yet no merchandise was placed in the windows.

O'Clare had frosted the glass over with a beer and Epsom salts solution until only the middle portion was transparent. Through these openings the blizzard was raging—bleached corn flakes were kept swirling around by a concealed hairdryer. The display card read: "It's coming—sooner or later." Amplifiers carried the sound of howling winds.

The issue of motion, which was vigorously and at times even bitterly debated in letters and editorials in *Display World,* brought into relief a basic disagreement among displaymen, store management, and others concerning the relation of display to its audience. Traditional fashion displays tended to have highly exclusive airs, presenting images of ponderous propriety that were apparently intended to interest only an audience assumed to be very small in number. By contrast, O'Clare's blizzard and other theatrical displays beginning with the Dali windows of 1936 offered a kind of amenity or entertainment. While the main intent of these windows was still very definitely to promote store sales, if more obliquely, their message was expressed in an idiom that made the windows of more general interest. They were more actively a part of the modern city street in its aspect as "a constant demonstration of vitality," as Marcel Breuer described the urban street scene. O'Clare for one was keenly interested in popular reaction to his displays, and had his office under a glass-bricked area of the sidewalk so that he could gauge pedestrian response to the windows by the sound of footsteps overhead.

O'Clare's approach to display, which he directed at Lord & Taylor from 1929 to 1941, was basically architectural. The first of his many unusual windows was done experimentally, following Dorothy Shaver's observation around 1935 that display in general lacked an element of surprise. Miss Shaver was vice-president of Lord & Taylor at the time. The economy was just starting to recover from the Depression, and as the fashion industry looked for ways of stimulating business, writers spoke of "a new slant" in hats, "a new slant" in belts, and so on. However that catch-phrase got its start, it was literally a slant that O'Clare gave the Lord & Taylor windows. As one observer, the display manufacturer Albert Bliss, recalled: "Strange new ramps were devised. Sweaters and other apparel were thrown casually from these ramps. Great sweeps of mouline were draped from the ceiling and hats were pinned to this mouline. Regular forms and fixtures were discarded and new shapes were created."

DANA O'CLARE

*Dana O'Clare (left) oversees work on Lord
& Taylor display in later 1930s. Window
floor has been routinely lowered by
hydraulic lift into underground work
area. Courtesy Dana O'Clare.*

For a display of sportswear, which during the late thirties was becoming a more important factor in the American fashion market, O'Clare set up windows as a series of sailboats, each with a workable canvas sail. The floors, for which ship's decks had been accurately constructed, were pitched for a novelty effect that also provided passersby with a better view of what *Display World* called a "large and colorful variety of summer apparel, generously intermixed with sea-going paraphernalia and yachting journals."

As backgrounds for women's wear displays, O'Clare preferred to use curved panels, which he believed brought out the feminine lines of the figures and clothes. For other windows, architectural themes provided atmosphere; for a fur window series miniature building facades of Paris were made from wallboard in false perspective, then mounted on plywood squares, and hung tilted forward to one side from the lower part of the background wall in each window. The buildings were painted in grays and browns to suggest aging stonework. The background walls were a light blue with clouds and streaks of deeper blues. O'Clare also used the Lord & Taylor elevator window floors as a design element, as in a series called "Excitement on the Sidelines" for which huge, menacing figures of football players—more wallboard cutouts—towered from the lower floors to nearly the full height of the windows. Goal posts shown in these neatly flattened and compressed scenes hung on flat forms. A mannequin perched on the goal post looked like a miniature doll beside what *Display World* termed O'Clare's "mighty gridiron Goliaths."

Among the most publicized and admired displays ever produced were O'Clare's Christmas bell windows of 1937 (see description, page 31). *Women's Wear Daily,* which had closely followed window display trends since the late twenties, reported that the store's decision to hold over the bell windows for several weeks was "quite unprecedented in retailing annals." The following spring, The Galeries Lafayette in Paris presented O'Clare's bell displays in its windows for Easter, the first and perhaps the only time a display of this kind has gone on tour. The bells were seen again at Lord & Taylor the following Christmases to 1941.

The Fifth Avenue Association did not try to prohibit the use of sound for display as it had the use of motion. O'Clare had produced the sound of the bells through amplifiers, as he had the sound of the blizzard. One wonders what the association's members thought about an O'Clare Valentine's Day display of 1938 for which perfume was sprayed into the air over each window so that, as *Display World* reported, "it was gently wafted to passersby, thus bringing them into intimate contact with the windows and appealing to a sense not reached by the ordinary display." As for the question of motion, the trade journal concluded that the theatrical type of display of which motion was sometimes an element "made not only the store's customers conscious of display as a vital, interesting factor in selling merchandise, but the general public, the store's employees, and the trade."

JIM BUCKLEY

We have Jim Buckley's shopping list for a set of window displays that he designed during the late thirties called "Elegantes in Birches." "New York," he writes, "was scoured for the following: one life-size horse; one well-head, large enough to hold a mannequin; one garden fountain; one baroque Venetian lamp; one peacock; one toadstool, seven feet high; three ancient musical instruments; three hundred pounds of gravel; one fawn; two tanks of water; eighty yards of rayon plush; one rowboat; two swans; five hundred butterflies, beetles and bugs; a profusion of quince blossoms; a troupe of wire women covered with birch-bark; signs, colored slides; three hundred and fifty square feet of grass especially grown for floor coverings. As for the pair of swans, as none of the taxidermists or museums in town could supply these protected birds, they had to be freshly slain so that the show might go on."

With that last macabre touch Buckley is winking at us. But then, the ability to transform a merely informative scene, however interesting in itself, into a theatrical gesture of surprising point and unity is a hallmark of Buckley's remarkable display work of the thirties, forties, and fifties. Buckley was display director at various stores in New York City, including I. Miller and Bergdorf Goodman, and at Saks Fifth Avenue in Beverly Hills.

In 1953, Buckley published a book, *The Drama of Display,* in which he outlined a variety of basic display techniques, often relating them by analogy to other forms of communication and to familiar, everyday sights and occurrences. His description of display as a design medium is unusual for its scope and idealism: "There is theater in display in more than its use of three-dimensional settings. It is there in the use of literary ideas objectified, communicated. In the mere fact of its being so prominent on the American landscape—in the visual expression of all lands where the individual is catered to—window display is part of the soul and substance of our philosophical and moral heritage. As a constantly constructive stimulus to better living it has a most welcome usefulness; not alone in promoting the products of a healthy industry but in simply adding to a pleasurable environment."

The treatment of a display idea, Buckley says, is always personal, but the ideas themselves do tend to be repeated. As a catalog of such ideas, *The Drama of Display* is extensive.

In Buckley's display work there was a sharp play back and forth between objects used as symbols and words. Often in a display, as in a rhebus, pictures or objects were substituted for, and made to be *read*, as words. Often Buckley seems to have started with a popular saying or expression and taken it to an absurd—literal, objectified—extreme.

To the lovers' old swoon, "We're alone at last," Buckley added, "dreaming and dining in the desert," seating a couple in evening dress on the ground beside a tall cactus in evening light. Oddly enough, the apparent light source was not the moon but a crystal chandelier, hanging in the middle of the desert. What was a chandelier doing there? It conveyed a "desirable note of elegance to point up the quality in the merchandise and to counterpoint the rustic setting," according to Buckley. Elsewhere in *The Drama of Display*, he remarks, "Personal idiosyncrasies, tendencies in one direction or another will sprout without forcing them." The rare authority of Buckley's windows arose largely from just such an insistence that the most bizarre or theatrical twist have an inherent purpose in terms of display technique and craft.

Among Buckley's main concerns as a displayman was creating a feeling of movement in windows, not by obvious mechanical means but through economy of design and with drama. This had a parallel for him in the working method of improvisation.

Objects and materials readily available to displaymen might, for instance, be turned into props of sudden grace and theatricality. Sectioned plaster mannequin molds were used by Buckley as floating sculptures in a series of windows called "Cast of Characters." In each window a mannequin in the store's clothes was surrounded by portions of the plaster forms from which the figure had once emerged—a ghostly and beautiful inverse anatomy, framing and drawing attention to the clothes. In another series, dress racks became fabulous skeletal window fixtures. Another week, transparent plastic coat hangers tied shoulder to shoulder and hung in rows across the length of a window were transformed into airy background scrims. An egg was suspended in a hairnet from the center of each hanger in these windows to give "weight" to the composition, Buckley says.

Anatomical analogies recurred in Buckley's windows. The idea of the frame, a related concept, was also very important. Picture frames (which are themselves really display fixtures) abstract and help give focus to the picture placed inside their borders, and in display the window itself is a kind of frame for the store's merchandise. Buckley put the frame analogy to further use as part of the actual design of certain displays, as in a fashion revival window for which he showed two mannequins, one a period figure in period clothes similar to those on which the new dress, worn by a contemporary mannequin, had been based. The older figure stood behind, and the modern figure stood in front of an ornate antique frame that could be read equally as framing a picture, a window, a mirror. A cellophane scrim across the frame gave the old-fashioned mannequin the appearance of an apparition, from which attention all but inevitably turned towards the store's new dress.

The appeal in most of Buckley's windows was expressly visual. A window card or sign might help unravel a more-or-less brilliant play on objects and words, but only after the visual image had created interest. Occasionally, a word became the image. For a series of Easter windows, Buckley made tall letters, one to a window, spelling "EASTER" in Victorian tangled-vine italics, with the letters doubling as fixtures on which mannequins were seated, gift items hung or otherwise placed, and various details added for festive touches of color and activity. Intertwined with the branches of the first letter E, for instance, was a garden hose, the nozzle hanging down from the top of the upper E curve, with water running lightly down from it into a bowl with fresh Easter lilies. Eggs were scattered across the window floors.

Eggs, hands, and eyes are among the images that often turned up in Buckley's displays: the egg, a symbol of fertility?—very possibly; the eye to catch other eyes; the hand as emblematic not only of craftsmanship—the made object—but also of "indication," the word by which Buckley sums up the purpose of display as an activity of pointing to and of pointing out.

Among the most memorable displays ever staged in New York was a series by Buckley and his assistant Robert Riley at Bergdorf Goodman in 1937. These were the "Chopin windows," done to coincide with a concert performance of the Chopin cycle by the pianist Alexander Brailousky. Grand piano bodies and piano skeletal parts were the main props. The magic of these windows lay in Buckley's ambitious attempt to make music visible through them. The transformation of sound into sight was accomplished—appropriately enough for a window display — by having the merchandise, which in this case consisted of flowing gowns that were placed on mannequins shaped out of actual sheet music—take on the elusive, central role.

Mannequins rose, "like music," from a musical source, the pianos. Gracefulness in the design was essential. In "Fantasie," a grand piano without legs was placed lengthwise on the window floor, lid raised. One mannequin was seen just emerging, head and shoulders, from inside the piano, arms raised in a dancer's gesture. Just overhead and off to the side, a full-length figure appeared in a gown draped as if in motion. A few small accessories were scattered here and there on and near the floor. And a "nest" of ferns, apparently growing out of the piano, concealed the sight line along the piano opening, so that the half-mannequin and the piano did not appear to be structurally part of each other, since the desired illusion was one of effortless upward musical flight. The absence of piano legs, Buckley notes, was not intended to add to the window's strangeness but rather was a case of editing to establish a clear vantage point for passing viewers. The background consisted of a curtain partly drawn off center.

There was considerable variety in Buckley's display work. "Situation display"—a term found in Buckley's book—and a style of display seen all around the country during the early seventies, is just one among many techniques described and illustrated in *The Drama of Display*. Buckley used it from time to time in his windows. In Buckley's displays, there was always a central idea informing the design, an idea which, as in the Chopin windows, satisfied the merchandising requirement of the window, but which also had an aesthetic interest of its own. Buckley, during his display career, was a leading advocate of the idea that display can be practiced at the level of an art. His best windows showed that commercial art may be designed to an aesthetic standard that is not in itself commercial.

HENRY F. CALLAHAN

Probably no one during the last forty years has done more in ready-to-wear display than Henry F. Callahan.

As display director of Lord & Taylor starting in late 1941, Callahan turned the store's four main display windows into a gala theater of high social occasion, fantasy, and fashion romance in which passersby caught glimpses of the lives, as Callahan says, of "the most fabulous people in the world." In the forties and fifties, "everyone wanted to be sophisticated," and this was reflected in the stylish formality with which people in the city dressed for work, the theater, or window-shopping. Lord & Taylor's windows were models of sophistication as well as entertainment in which realism was a key—realism in the mannequins, in the way they were posed, and in the stage settings. Even when the setting was itself a fantasy—a Mississippi riverboat or the caverns of a dreamscape made entirely of coal—the detail was elaborate. Mannequins were involved in a subtle play of glances and posturing that was all dramatic suggestion—all half-told tales for the viewer to fill in or imagine. Every day large crowds gathered to see the displays, to an extent that only happens now at Christmas.

Under the direction of Dorothy Shaver, vice-president and later president of Lord & Taylor, the entire store management was display-conscious and an unusual rapport existed among those responsible for the various forms of store advertising and promotion. They met together regularly to exchange ideas, and at one time Callahan had a set of mannequins designed based on Dorothy Hood's fashion sketches for the store's ads. An influence on Callahan from outside the store was Cecil Beaton, whose sketches and writings as well as his photographs for *Vogue* presented an ongoing portrait of society life such as Callahan also created in his windows.

During World War II, Callahan says, he "never let the sadness of the war take away from the glamor of the windows. Men came home on leave. Many women doing various kinds of wartime service wore uniforms during the day and when they got home at night they wanted to put on something very feminine." Stores that provided these clothes at a moderate price, including Lord & Taylor, became symbols of well-being, of which the windows were outward signs.

Wartime rationing of materials did not particularly limit Callahan's staging of unusual displays. "There were always flowers, there were always fabrics, there were always antiques around." And most of the propping and scenery, including grand stairways, balconies at the opera, terraces and room interiors, were built in the store's work-shop—on a shoestring, often contrary to their appearance of great cost. The finished settings were then lifted into place on the windows' elevator platform floors, which Callahan often also used as part of the setting.

The Lord & Taylor windows' elevator floors were installed in 1914, probably intended more as a mechanical aid than as a device for window theater, since display in 1914 was not often very theatrical. Dana O'Clare, under whom Callahan first worked at the store, some-times used the floors to advantage from an architectural display standpoint, but Callahan played them for dramatic illusion, setting up as many as four different levels on which action might be staged.

The 1949 Lord & Taylor Christmas windows, "The Lights of Christ-mas," were Renaissance-inspired interpretations of various lights as-sociated symbolically with the holiday. In one window, "The Firelight of Christmas," an 8-foot tall figure in Renaissance costume, appar-ently covered with glowing coals and flames, stood in front of a parted curtain in a window. This was the "Spirit of Firelight": the curtain was made of red china silk and was kept in constant motion by concealed fans; lighted to give an effect of dancing flames. Looking in through the curtain, passersby saw a family of the Renaissance gathered around the hearth. Strangely, they appeared to be far off in the distance, and were in fact located well below street level. What spectators actually saw was a mirror reflection of the scene, set up by Callahan on a lowered elevator platform.

There was remarkable variety in the windows from week to week. In March 1947, Callahan made plaster murals as backgrounds for a set of windows—considered an unusual technique for display then—which *Display World* said gave the windows "a very French air." The design for one window was of cupids and aerial balloons bearing flowers, all done in high relief in papier-mâché, plaster, and paint applied in a thick impasto. The cupids were painted with black masks, chokers, ballet slippers, and instead of painted wings, tufts of real pink and white feathers sprouted from the plaster walls. The cupids' hair was of unraveled rope and excelsior. Some of the balloons were striped pink and white, and the largest was crowned with ostrich feathers. As a finishing touch all the floors were covered with pink and lavender pebbles.

About a month after the mural windows, Callahan did a series in which the four main windows were transformed into coal grottoes with pillars and arches of coal. The floor was gleaming white satin; the fashion copy was scrawled on it with coal. Cecilia Staples, whose display studio built part of the settings for the windows from Callahan's sketches, had for some time been considering the display possibilities of coal when Callahan called her with an actual plan. Staples made various shapes in papier-mâché which were covered with coal particles. A special glue had to be mixed for this purpose. "The real mineral," *Display World* noted, "was used wherever possible so that the overall effect was completely that of coal." Mannequins dressed in black gowns were posed in these settings of "weird mystic beauty," as the trade journal called them.

In other windows, interest centered almost entirely on the clothes, as in a series of 1953 in which Anne Fogarty's "Paper Doll" look dresses were first shown publicly (see page 116). These dresses represented a radical departure in fashion from the last fifty years, during which most dresses had been pencil thin and petticoats were thought of as Victorian. Callahan placed a simple banner headline across the top of the window with the name "Anne Fogarty" and in one window had two metallic palm trees as sophisticated bits of stage-setting. One figure stood off to the side in the older, narrow type of dress. All across the rest of the window stood a grouping of mannequins in the new Anne Fogarty's. Hundreds of passersby stopped to see these displays. To show off all the petticoats, Callahan used mirrored floors.

After leaving Lord & Taylor in 1956, Callahan worked briefly for Schenley, redesigning their packaging. Later that year, he went to Saks Fifth Avenue, where he was vice president and corporate director of visual presentation until 1977. There he went towards greater simplicity in the windows, often using only one mannequin in a display and sometimes none at all. The Phantom, first seen in New York at the specialty shop Hattie Carnegie, but developed considerably by Callahan, made its appearance in Saks' windows during the midsixties, when clothes were highly tailored. The absence of an actual mannequin (clothes were wired into the shape of a standing figure, hung in place in the window with accessories also hung in place—a hat here, a raised glove there) accentuated the crisp lines of the clothes. The Phantom had great sophistication and was seen by people at the time as an acknowledgment of the fact that "the women we were appealing to," as Callahan says, "knew who they were. They didn't need to see an actual figure." The Phantom idea also worked because women at that time wore hats and gloves, which became visual clues to The Phantom's whereabouts in the windows.

Because the windows at Saks are relatively shallow, especially when compared with those at Lord & Taylor, Callahan used black backgrounds so that the rear walls would recede into space. In some windows, light was used not only to bring out the clothes but also as a complete dramatic setting. One series, done with The Phantom against a background of strings of Christmas lights, was an apotheosis of the glamor of the city after dark. In 1957, for the fiftieth anniversary celebration of The Fifth Avenue Association, Callahan did a series of windows in gold. The midtown skyline was recreated in miniature, building for building, on the window floors with scale models done in metal by Guy Miller. In one window, according to the *Display World* account, "a graceful mannequin in a pleated golden gown seemed to hover like a golden spirit about the magic, metal skyline. Her scarf was a soft, golden shade, the ribbons around her waist were golden toned, her gloves were pale beige, and her jewelry of rhinestones." The window floor was black, scattered with bits of gold. Spotlighting produced a glowing aura around the figure, and light rising from inside the miniature buildings added to a double illusion of realism and fantasia that cohered in the window because it was done with style.

Many of Callahan's innovations in display methods and techniques occurred to him as second nature in response to a specific need. Once many years ago when mannequins were stood on platforms in the windows, Callahan and his staff found a mannequin whose legs could not be lined up to be attached to the base. He discarded the platform and suspended wires between the mannequin and the floor to hold the figure in place. This eventually became the technique used everywhere in display.

Callahan, who has opened a consulting firm based in Philadelphia, has always been considered an authority on fashion as well as on display and other matters of decor and taste. His display work was represented at The Museum of Modern Art's twentieth anniversary show "Modern Art in Your Life." His breadth of expertise enhanced not only his own position at the stores where he worked, but also that of display directors generally. Among his related activities, he has trimmed the White House Christmas tree, done store windows in Paris, and designed for many gala events and occasions. The world he has depicted in his windows is very much the world in which he has worked and lived. Photographs of Callahan's windows are as telling a record as any of what society has meant over forty years by such words as fashion, elegance, taste, style, and glamor.

Henry F. Callahan, Saks Fifth Avenue, New York, 1965. Photograph by Malan Studio, Inc., New York. Courtesy Saks Fifth Avenue.

GENE
MOORE

"There are so many things that can be beautiful that people don't really see. You look at it. You pass it by. It's a commonplace thing. I love commonplace things. I love to make people *see* commonplace things."

An unusually receptive eye for beauty in its various forms has always characterized the design work of Gene Moore, display director of Tiffany & Company since 1955. Moore, in displaying fine jewelry and other objects of accepted beauty, has eliminated all pretense, showing that beauty is less rare than people have often imagined. Eggshells, rope, dirt, paper, water, and grass have all been seen in his displays as appropriate foils for jeweler's artistry, each with visual character of its own. Seashells, light bulbs, fresh flowers, toy dolls, artist's modeling figures (see page 147), and carpenter's nails have all been sources of display to Moore, whose work has often held an element of surprise for passersby as well as for fellow displaymen. Concerning public response, Tom Lee, writing in *Graphis* in 1960, remarked that "New York considers the work of Gene Moore one of its main visual ornaments."

Many artists and craftsmen have shown their work in Moore's windows at Tiffany. Jasper Johns, Robert Rauschenberg, and Andy Warhol worked for him at Bonwit Teller during the fifties, and some of the first major public exhibitions of Pop Art were staged not in a gallery or museum, but in Bonwit Teller's windows as part of the week's displays.

Moore himself was represented by windows in The Museum of Modern Art's twentieth anniversary show "Modern Art in Your Life," and he has also designed jewelry exhibitions for museums. In addition he has designed jewelry for Tiffany, where he is also a vice president. Moore has worked as a portrait photographer and has done fashion photographs that he used as background settings in his windows. Dance has been a theme of windows by Moore for displays of shoes, dresses, and jewelry, and he has also designed sets and costumes for The Paul Taylor Dance Company. In these and other ways, display work for Gene Moore has been related to other forms of design and the arts.

As in fine photography, his display work reveals an individual, highly developed awareness of light and its expressive qualities. As in dance and graphic art, Moore's energetic handling of pattern, mass, imagery, and line implies a drama of movement and protean change. A wooden spool, an abandoned gargoyle, a hat pin, or a feather—anything that is "good design"—is as likely to be taken as a prop by Moore and his assistant Ron Smith as is an object of more accepted beauty.

The main element in Moore's window displays is not the prop or the jewelry but the balance between them—a balance expressed in terms of a visual analogy, a play on words as objects and objects as words, or some other dramatic idea or perception that results in a window—often at the last minute, Moore says.

The balance of a window becomes an invisible third term, and viewers are called on to complete the picture.

"Some people look at the windows," Moore sighs, "and all they see is the jewelry."

Other people like to find mistakes. Once for a display of flatware,

Moore lined up rows of knives, forks, and spoons in the window all of the same pattern, except for one fork half-hidden in a corner (see page 153). Many passersby came into the store to point out the "error."

"I can do a window with letters or postcards," Moore says. "Even if I put them in upside down, people will stand there and *read them*. If they are printed, no. But in handwriting, yes. Then it's somebody's personal writing. Don't you find that odd?"

Such windows, with their traces of "that lovely evil thing" that Moore admires in the work of Alfred Hitchcock, may rely on a viewer's willingness to stop longer than usual for a display. But in general, Moore prefers windows in which a message is rapidly communicated, especially when for that brief second or two the window actively engages the viewer beyond the point of merely saying, "Oh, that's nice." A display that comments on a current event may draw looks of recognition from passersby. It may express a common feeling. During an unusually hot summer, for instance, Moore took advantage of "ice"—the jewel thief's term for diamonds—setting one of the store's diamonds in a pair of ice tongs beside a large, very cool-looking block of ice. During a water shortage in the city, Moore designed windows with fountains not of water but recirculating gin. When there was a serious transit strike that had many people more quick-tempered than usual (many more people were walking than usual), Moore's recommended alternate means of transportation—rollerskates, unicycle (see page 151), pogo stick—were all suggestions that produced many a smile.

Display, Moore says, is a medium in which a merchandising point is often an important part, but always only a part of what is being communicated. While he is less concerned with merchandising at Tiffany than he was as display director of Bonwit Teller (from 1945 to 1962), at Delman and Bergdorf Goodman (during the late 1930s and early 1940s), and other stores where he has at times worked, his manner of addressing his audience has always been the same. "The first thing you have to do in display is make people stop. But I won't go to outside limits to make them stop. I'm not going to scream and yell at them. I'm going to whisper it to them. I think so much more can be done by whispering than by yelling. So much advertising and promotion is such yelling. Like TV commercials. They're talking down to everyone. I can't stand that. I never play down. I always play up. I think it's even wrong in raising a child to play down. Otherwise, what do you do for the child? You don't raise it. I think it's absolutely wrong. I feel the same way about windows."

Working with miniatures—playing with scale—Moore has given the Tiffany windows an unexpected quality of fantasia. Miniatures often take on a seemingly magical interest in everyday life, as for instance bonsai and certain children's toys sometimes do. Jewelry, which is often associated with fantasy (the wearing of jewelry is a form of display), is seen in high relief when related to a setting of miniature scale.

Moore, while doing the sets for a John Gielgud production, once told a skeptical stage designer that a window display is not a miniature theater; a stage set is really a large window display. And while, as

Moore is well aware, stage and display work actually involve very different sets of limitations, the visual concerns of the designers are often much the same. To create a convincing illusion of depth in a shadowbox, for example, some means must be found to make viewers willing to forget the window's actual dimensions. Stage designers are often faced with a similar task. In Moore's windows, light is a key to the illusion.

For most displays, a fluorescent light is placed in a trough in the floor along the back wall of each window. The light source is below the viewer's eye level. A cool white light rises a short distance up along the felt window lining. Fluorescent light does not project far from its source, and the effect is of a glowing aura along the lower edge of the back wall for backlighting. In a window that has been designed with, say, a paper toy castle on a low mountain ledge with a gold pin of a man standing in the foreground, this rim of light for the enchanted viewer suddenly becomes the earth's horizon (see page 144).

Gene Moore, Tiffany & Co., New York, 1971. Photograph by Malan Studio, Inc., New York. Courtesy Malan Studio, Inc.

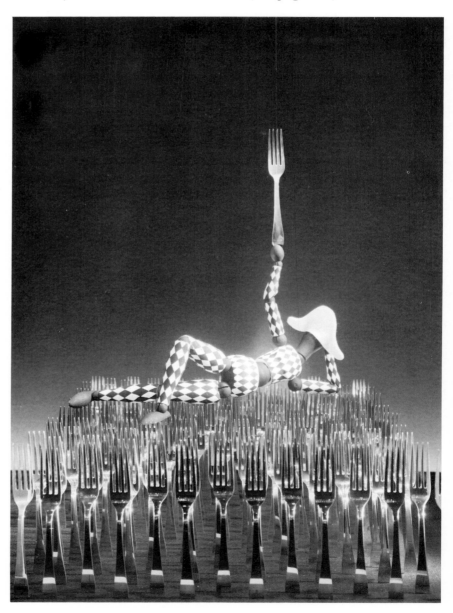

Moore's display career began with a job making artificial flowers in an artificial flower show. There, he met Jim Buckley, who asked him to become his assistant at I. Miller. Moore next became Delman's display director in the late thirties. He still refers to himself as a "window trimmer." The basic modesty of his work consists of Moore's high respect for craftsmanship of the simplest as well as the most elaborate kinds and in an unassuming attitude towards both audience and materials.

Moore has designed various other windows around New York, including the window at the Madison Avenue Bookshop, for which he invented a dapper character whose purpose in life, as a regular feature at the store, is curiously like that of an old-fashioned cigar-store Indian (see page 54).

"That figure is a nineteenth-century religious figure, carved wood, with movable limbs. He's really a work of art. I wanted something that is immediately identifiable with the shop. And I think to use him in a different way each time the window is changed creates an interest in him. What is he going to do next? So I have great fun with him. He is my friend. He helps me. I love him. I think it's a good merchandising idea to give something to people they want to come back and see. And suddenly if it goes on month after month they're going to become aware of him. I'm very aware of him. I say, 'Christ, what am I going to make him do now?'"

Moore often has several design projects under way in addition to the Tiffany windows. He would like someday to stage classic children's fairy tales for television. But display is the work that he has been continually dedicated to for more than forty years. He enjoys having total control over the design of his windows, and he enjoys the windows' temporariness. "I can make it funny. I can make it beautiful. I can make shock. I can't make it sad. Display is magic exactly as theater is magic and should be more so than it is. It becomes too obvious. I'm too aware of all the tricks. There are so many unexplained things in the world. Each person has fantasy. It's beautiful. Who's to say it's real or not real. I don't know. Do you?"

Gump's in San Francisco is among the few stores that people from around the world visit as they would a gallery or museum. As a store known for merchandise of excellent design, Gump's represents a sort of commercial other-side-of-the-coin to various museums, including The Museum of Modern Art in New York, insofar as these cultural institutions have acknowledged an aesthetic dimension to commercial design and have also begun selling various products of this kind to the public in their own museum shops.

A store with consistently high standards for its merchandise is as apt a setting as a museum in which to find evidence of a rapport between the fine and applied arts. When commercial products are especially well designed, it is to be hoped that they will be made available through stores to the public. Since the 1940s, Gump's has also had merchandise displays, notably in its windows, that are themselves works of applied art of comparable quality to the store's merchandise. According to Robert Mahoney, Gump's display director since 1963, the windows are largely based on principles of Oriental art and design

ROBERT MAHONEY

because most of the store's goods are imported from the Far East. Gump's displays and merchandise thus complement each other as illustrations of the same or similar aesthetics.

Probably the main idea that Gump's windows express is that elegance is a form of simplicity. Mahoney's concern as display director has been with presenting merchandise with increasing simplicity, showing objects in a way that is closer to museum display than is usually seen in store windows. Visually, the main difference between store and museum presentation is that a store window must do more to call attention to itself. Often by minimal means, Mahoney has related the various objects in a window to each other with a sense of graphic focus and theater. Props and merchandise, like actors, seem to point each other out in the displays.

Simplicity is shown in Gump's windows in the choice and handling of materials. The window walls are made of ordinary plywood, painted white during the year and a different color each Christmas. Once when scraping down the boards to prepare them for repainting, Mahoney cut through eight layers of color—"eight Christmases," he says. "It was like counting the rings of a tree."

With walls and floors left mainly bare, the few objects placed in a window—china, glass, jade, silver, cloth, or paper—stand in relief with poster clarity. Light and a feeling of airy spaciousness are maximized by these otherwise neutral surfaces. The side walls slant inward toward the back; the floors are raked forward in a false perspective illusion. The windows look deeper as objects in them are brought forward towards the viewer.

Display ideas, design elements, color scheme all come out of the merchandise Mahoney has to work with in a given week. He has, for instance, shown fish-shaped baking dishes in a setting of wooden pilings and paper waves. An assortment of china led to the idea of building a Nevelsonesque cabinet sculpture in which all the plates and vases could be placed. Commercial display props are rarely used—partly to keep down expenses, partly to avoid overcomplicating the window style.

Mahoney has on staff one of the few people he knows who can do by hand all the sign painting and lettering needed for the windows. A fragment of calligraphy or a bit of handwriting has at times been made into the main design element of a display, as when black posterboard was curved up onto the back of a window with three glass objects placed in front and with prices marked in chalk on the black backing. Radical in its simplicity, the window was a triumph, and Mahoney feels that evidence of hand work is essential to his displays, not only because the merchandise is similarly crafted, but also because it becomes a reflection of the store's individuality.

In a window design, Mahoney finds "the odd number more interesting. The use of five objects instead of six. The use of odd-numbered objects instead of even relationships between objects. The Japanese see more interest in an odd grouping. Balancing the use of negative space to balance an object, not symmetrically, not object for object, but mass for mass."

Humor comes readily to Mahoney, but it will work in a display, he says, only if viewers see it rapidly, "in two seconds or less. It must work even faster than billboard advertising." Comedy, alas, even arises out of Mahoney's resourcefulness in the face of a relatively limited display budget. Although he rarely uses standard mannequins, for instance, he is fond of flat plywood cut-outs that he makes himself and that can at times give a light touch to a window just by not being the usual, more elaborately gotten-up figure. Once for a dress sale, Mahoney drew a group of life-size figures on the walls, pinning the clothes flat against these two-dimensional models (see page 132). The floor was left completely bare except for a set of large paper cut-out letters spelling "SALE." The playful, last-minute style of handling the window (which required considerable artistry) set the tone for a clearance.

"I like to do the magical thing," Mahoney says. He enjoys working with a transparent plastic display wire that allows him to have tables, playing cards, soup tureens all appear to float in space. Mahoney is also one of the few American displaymen to employ illusions of scale in large-scale display windows. (German and Swiss designers have also done this.) Once, for instance, he built a large wedding cake from the floor up, with each tier serving as a tabletop, ornamented with silk roses and a selection of the store's china.

Mahoney tries, however, to avoid getting carried away by the magic to the point of making the merchandise look better than it really is. He once did a window with bookends in two-color glass that were shaped like apples. Mahoney had a barrel of the apples with the barrel split open and the apples spilling out, all lighted from beneath. The apples glowed brilliantly and sold very well. "Then people got them home and put them on a bookshelf or something and the apples just sat there. All the apples came right back to the store."

Works of art have been shown in a variety of ways in window display, as props—to suggest a period setting, atmosphere, or decor—or as a visual complement to merchandise of fine quality. But in his windows,

Robert J. Mahoney, Gump's, San Francisco, mid-1960s. Photograph by Davis. Courtesy Gump's.

Mahoney often deals with art as merchandise. Few other display directors have had the daring or the skill to do this effectively. Here the question of whether display is itself an art is brought into sharpest focus, since the merchandise, if it is a fine work of art, sets an exquisite standard that the setting may enhance but must not violate, while also presenting it for sale to passersby.

For a display of Ben Shahn graphics, Mahoney strung the window with a light network of crisscrossing black threads that attracted attention from a distance and that related to Shahn's characteristic line without detracting from the pictures. Even simpler means were resorted to for a display of Oriental stone figure carvings. Dramatic spotlighting, an elegant but plain hand-lettered sign, and the placement of the objects were the only design elements brought into play.

Mahoney handles each object in his windows with a basic respect for materials. Paper is paper, dirt is dirt, crystal is crystal. This is perhaps a key to the unassuming elegance of Gump's windows.

HOWARD NEVELOW

Once while Howard Nevelow, display director of the Delman Shoe Salon in New York, was going for a walk, he saw a heavy plate glass door suddenly collapse for no apparent reason, shattering into thousands of small, bead-shaped pieces. No one was injured in the accident, and as workmen swept up the debris, Nevelow had an idea. He asked the workman not to throw away the glass and took it back to his office where he designed and built a series of three miniature ice palaces from the fragments. These became the settings for the following week's window displays at Delman.

Metal shoehorns, of which Nevelow has a ready supply, became the leaves of a Christmas wreath and the boughs of a Christmas tree one year in Delman's windows (see page 156). Delman shoes have been little boats, each with a raised paper sail in a sea of paper waves in the windows. Shoes have been snowbound in miniature drifts of snow with long columns of tiny penguins marching all around them. Shoes have also appeared on toy parade floats, as apparitions in a field of miniature windmills, and as gondolas on real water before photomurals of Venice (see pages 160–161), among other roles and settings in Nevelow's displays.

The range of analogies that have occurred to Nevelow in displaying shoes is remarkable. Some of his windows—the toy boat display, for example, or another in which pairs of shoes were seen as butterfly wings (see page 159)—would interest linguists and mythologists, one suspects, as well as passersby who look mainly at the shoes.

Playing with the visual scale of things, as Nevelow has done in many windows, is, as Lewis Carroll, the surrealists, and others have shown, a way of engaging a viewer's sense of fantasy. And while in commercial display this or any other device as a means of pointing to a store's merchandise might easily become cute or precious or heavyhanded, Nevelow's window miniatures and giants have, by contrast, had the poignancy of fine craftsmanship applied to modest ends. One is reminded of the toymakers and cobblers of children's fairytales when seeing some of the props and window decorations that Nevelow has made or had made for him out of such everyday objects and materials as pencils, flashlight reflectors, foot pads (see pages 162–163), postage stamps, slats of glass. But Nevelow's windows are at the same time very sophisticated, and it is often through an unexpected play between the makeshift and more polished types of beauty that his displays have had an aesthetic validity of their own.

The parade float windows, with their daftly hokey miniversions of an almost vanished form of public spectacle and display, had a camp aura of nostalgia about them. Other windows involving plays on scale have had a surreal quality.

Nevelow once designed a series of displays that were directly based on paintings by René Magritte (see page 158). In each window, some object pictured in the original painting was replaced by a shoe. In Nevelow's version of "The Castle of the Pyrenees," for example, a shoe was seen in place of the castle that stands atop a huge rock which floats in space above a shoreline. The windows might well have been coy or pretentious, but they succeeded not only as "good fakes," but also as surrealist minor variations on the original theme. The bizarre, looming quality of the shoes was largely, of course, but not entirely defused by the context of the images: their sales role. But the windows were also quite beautiful in their own right and perhaps also somewhat disturbing in surrealist terms, although surrealism's range of emotional concerns is one that display as a commercial medium is really very limited in treating.

Nevelow in his windows has always shown a sense of theater, and he has worked with at least two regular characters at various times during his display career. As the display director at the specialty shop Hattie Carnegie during the fifties, Nevelow introduced The Phantom to New York. A dress, hat, gloves, and other accessories were all wired into place in a natural standing position on their imaginary wearer—no mannequin was actually seen. Sometimes photo blow-ups filled in the missing person, and for one series, Dovima, one of the leading models of the fifties, posed for the pictures, an arm here, a leg there, and above all the unforgettable face—each element framed separately in gold and carefully fitted to complete the composition (see page 127).

At Delman one Easter during the early sixties, Nevelow had a troupe of three rabbits, one for each window, made by the display studio of Staples-Smith. The rabbits were designed to scale as specified by Nevelow, who also asked that the rabbits have no ears. Shoes, it had occurred to him, look something like rabbit ears, and pairs of Delman shoes thus became the wacky but somehow also very elegant finishing details of these festive creatures, which reappeared at Easter for many years, each time cast in a different situation that related to current events in the city or around the world.

During the New York World's Fair in 1965, Nevelow took one of the Delman rabbits out to the fairgrounds, dressed it with shoe ears and a tourist outfit complete with toy camera, and photographed the little hero on the central lawn in front of the Unisphere, the fair's symbol. The photograph became the background for a window in which the actual rabbit also appeared on a miniature lawn set up on the window floor in a trompe l'oeil illusion that was pure confection.

"The rabbits took care of the need to display the shoes, so I was free

Howard Nevelow, Delman Shoe Salon, New York, 1965. Photograph by Malan Studio, Inc., New York. Courtesy Delman Shoe Salon.

to do anything I wanted with the rest of the window," Nevelow explains.

When "Harvey," a play featuring a giant rabbit, opened on Broadway, Nevelow and the Delman rabbits were ready for the occasion (see page 50). When American astronauts first landed on the moon, so did the Delman rabbits. In the year of the Chinese ping-pong exhibitions in the U.S., the Delman rabbits put on an Oriental face and turned up in the windows with paddles and a miniature table (see page 156). In other Easter windows, rabbits were seen filling out their tax returns, posing in front of Lincoln Center, at the Plaza (see page 157), in a cabbage patch, and in a pile of carrots.

In holding up shoes as ears, Nevelow displayed the shoes very clearly for passersby. In Nevelow's work generally, merchandise has not been lost in the shuffle, so to speak, of display theatricality. The theater is always there—in the idea of a window, in the analogy, and in the craft of pulling ice palaces out of a dust bin or the Delman rabbit out of a hat (see frontispiece).

ROBERT BENZIO

"The composition for me really begins," Robert Benzio, vice-president and director of visual presentation at Saks Fifth Avenue, says, "with the mannequin." Benzio places a figure or grouping of mannequins at the center of most of his windows. Although this in itself is a traditional strategy in ready-to-wear display, few if any displaymen operating on the scale of the large specialty store have so extensive a knowledge of display and other decorative arts traditions as does Benzio. While a great deal of current display strikes the eye as lacking in texture and continuity of ideas about design, Benzio has for many years drawn on both old and new sources to make a variety of contemporary statements in his windows.

Turn-of-the-century wax mannequins, with their antique doll colorings and finishes, appeal to him greatly as material: "I would love to do components or attitudes after them," he says. He generally prefers to work with realistic contemporary figures, but has also used futuristic mannequins with video screens on which the clothes on the figures could be seen in motion (see page 174). In some of his windows a prop has become an element of surprise, as when large metal fans were shown, with a classic grouping of mannequins, where flowers or vases on pedestals might have been expected (see page 51). Paintings, rugs, vases, furniture, and antiques of various kinds—all props that "everybody has used"—often appear in Benzio's windows, but not in the predictable context of a furnished room. A window bank is treated as a whole, along which Benzio and a staff of fifteen assistants present the clothes each week in several carefully thought-out and related variations on the overall "attitude" of the fashion season. The windows depict not a series of dramatic moments, but an atmosphere or ambiance in relation to which the beauty of the clothes is highlighted. The displays are texturally more subtle, dramatically more restrained than, say, the situation windows of the early seventies, including Benzio's. A bizarre or surreal quality is often present in his work, sometimes at a decorative level, sometimes as an element of drama.

Each season, Benzio, who has previously been display director at Best & Co., DiPinna, and B. Altman, all in New York, rethinks his style in terms of the clothes he will be showing. In 1977, when fashions were romantic, Benzio "went more opulent" in his displays, "but always with an element of control. We went through what we called our 'stripped palace' attitude. This was a set within a set. Rugs were never put on the floor. Rugs were always draped over something. Paintings were never hung on the wall. Paintings were left leaning against a wall or a piece of furniture. One of the first times this attitude became apparent was when I borrowed a tremendous amount of French furniture and I told the man that I wanted him to know I was going to cover most of it and I didn't want him to be upset. I had a set of peau de soie draperies made, and we literally just hung them in front of these chairs and paintings, and they were really just peeking out. The element of design was the drapery, not the furniture." Ballet provided a metaphor for displays of these romantic clothes, but as often as not, dancers were shown not in performance but in rehearsal or backstage.

With a "suggestion of snow on a parquet floor," Benzio has indicated winter (see page 172). In the same series of windows, large gold leaf picture frames appeared in the foreground, an unframed painting of clouds hung as background, and mannequins were posed in between, as if caught between illusions. Atmosphere had been created, with minimal means, yet there was a baroque quality, and all the rest of the walls were bare. "So you can see that it's contemporary and yet there's a romantic involvement. What's really contemporary is all that space," says Benzio. Following the "stripped palace" season, clothes became "a little more believable, less like costume. Softer, more sensual." In Benzio's windows, "pose became very important—that languid, reclining pose that we were one of the first to use (see page 173). We went away from ballet, away from petticoats and that kind of thing. I never used gold or silver leaf but lacquers and pecan woods. The walls were padded in fabric, and very definitely in a tactile kind of fabric. I felt that was very important, that there was a wonderful play of textures, between raw silks and linen, and things like that, because the clothes were gauze, linen, silk, raw silk, and you have to remember all that."

"Step windows" by Robert Benzio, Saks Fifth Avenue, New York, 1976. Photograph by Malan Studio, Inc., New York. Courtesy Saks Fifth Avenue.

Close-up of Benzio step window at Saks Fifth Avenue.

For Benzio during the latter season, Frank Lloyd Wright "became an inspiration because of his use of certain materials, water for instance; his idea of plantlife as connected with the building plane as a unit; the circular, curvilinear shapes as opposed to hard-edge straight lines." Similarly, during the stripped palace days, Benzio studied the work of the Mexican architect Luis Barragan: "With his use of stucco and color, he related so beautifully to what people were doing with an outdoor kind of spirit in clothing."

Barragan's buildings have a magical quality of seeming warm and familiar just when they are formally most abstract, an effect that Benzio experimented with in a bank of window settings with cloud backgrounds, tile rooftop floors, stucco walls, and natural wood interiors with skylights. Benzio prefers in general to color the window banks' long, usually bare walls not in white—as has been seen in many stores during the seventies—but in warm pastel colors, which make the windows more formal in tone, but also more intimate.

Passersby who know Wright's or Barragan's work would not necessarily have recognized their influence in Benzio's displays, but to him this is unimportant. What he particularly disliked about some of the violent and shocking situation windows of the early seventies was the "obviousness" of their statement. In surrealism, it is not the shock quality that Benzio finds useful in his own work, but a purity of forms. "There is romance and a dream quality connected to surrealism. I consider myself a romantic. But there is always this sparse, this wonderful feeling of space and horizon." Surrealism then, as it relates to his treatments of window space, has a basically architectural meaning.

Among Benzio's best displays at Saks Fifth Avenue from the standpoint of drama and of the publicity it drew to the store was the "step window" series, for which, working with false perspective, the illusion was formed of an unbroken staircase spanning the entire length of the central Fifth Avenue window bank and receding far into the distance. The staircase, although seen behind the glass, appeared to be a monumental architectural setting, like the outer staircase of the Forty-Second Street Library or The Metropolitan Museum of Art. A mannequin, dressed in the store's furs, was seen on the steps in each window, apparently on the way out from whatever building the staircase led to. The display was set in an evening light. The phantom architecture of the massive steps introduced an element of mystery that left the figure in each window nonetheless clearly visible at the center of an uncluttered picture.

While many people would probably expect to see unusual merchandise unusually displayed in the store windows of, say, New York and San Francisco, it is perhaps more surprising that some of the finest display work currently being done anywhere in the United States is to be found in Salt Lake City at ZCMI, where Ron Nelson is visual merchandising director.

RON NELSON

ZCMI (Zion's Cooperative Mercantile Institution), which was founded in 1868, is considered the oldest department store in the United States. Display at the store may once have had a peculiarly religious significance for its founders and original owners and customers belonged to The Mormon Church, which tends to view material prosperity as a sign of spiritual well-being. While the Mormons remain stockholders in the store, both ZCMI and the city in which it operates have become heterogeneous and more cosmopolitan, according to Nelson. There are now several other department stores in town. And display serves the same purpose at ZCMI as it does at other stores where it is practiced with a high degree of artistry and care, as a way of advertising the store's merchandise, and as a means of making the store itself more inviting to customers.

Nelson, who has overall responsibility for window and interior display at ZCMI's six branch stores in and around the Salt Lake City area, has a staff of thirty-five designers and workers. While avoiding formulas in his designs, Nelson has organized his department in what seems like an unusually well-coordinated, systematic way.

ZCMI's display department has a workshop in which nearly all of the props and other decorations for the store's windows and interiors are designed and built. The shop is equipped for work with wood, metals, plastics as well as for silk-screening and sign painting. The materials and colors chosen for props and backgrounds are varied considerably. Often, for instance, deep or muted background colors that have a formal quality are played off against the spacious, contemporary graphic look of a window design. It seems probable that many people in the Salt Lake City area make a point of going by ZCMI's windows regularly to see what the designers are doing now.

Not all ZCMI's branch stores rely equally on window display, which is generally directed to pedestrians and so is less important (if not entirely absent) at suburban stores that customers enter directly from their cars. But Nelson notes a trend towards making more use of windows at suburban stores, and has done so at ZCMI, where windows have been placed at entranceways. These windows are used to call attention to various current features of the mall and to help create an atmosphere that is less like that of an anonymous airport, which is often suggested by the entrances to such shopping areas.

Fresh flowers are almost always seen around ZCMI's stores and are often also shown in the display windows. Flowers, like all decorations used for display at ZCMI, are for sale, and many customers leave the stores with flowers under their arms, often perhaps more to their own surprise than to Nelson's. Each item that appears in ZCMI's displays is kept track of by means of a central tagging system, so that if a vaseful of flowers or the vase catches the fancy of a customer, it can be taken out of the display for the customer and then rapidly replaced.

Among Nelson's varied resources is a display window at the main downtown store that is an unsegmented space more than 50 feet long. The window is well beyond the scale of an alcove or ordinary room, and some of the most visually pleasing displays done with it have been outdoor settings. A display of furs, for instance, was designed as a winter forest scene (see pages 194–195). The entire floor was covered with a deep layering of artificial snow, seen in cross-section through the glass. Tinted lights cast delicate accents of color onto the snow that were reflected upward across the expanse of the window. The mannequins were all grouped to one side. Standing trees and the negative space of the snow-covered forest floor completed the window, which was a remarkable fusion of lyric atmosphere and pared-down graphic design.

Nelson reports that he has had relatively little interference on religious grounds concerning what he does with his displays. But if he is planning a situation type of display, he usually does choose a situation that is not likely to cause much controversy with "extreme hellers." The snow forest window is an example of a display that most viewers probably would have found quite beautiful.

For another display in the long window, Nelson used a forties wooden stand-up telephone booth as the only prop. The phone booth, because of its age, had the interest of a kind of age-of-electronics antique. A large grouping of mannequins were arranged around it, apparently waiting to use the phone. While they were "waiting," they displayed a large number of the store's new dresses.

Nelson has many sizes and shapes of window to work with, as well as an unusual variety of merchandise. The store carries a large selection of designer clothes as well as less expensive clothing, and all the various types of goods typically found in department stores. ZCMI has also kept up some of its original general-store lines of stock, which gives Nelson a chance to design with many types of goods—hardware and fresh produce, for example—that are usually neglected for display. Rather than placing huge assortments of, say, wrenches and hammers in such a window, Nelson uses just a few items in an unlikely way—by combining various tools into an odd machine of his own invention, for example—which serves as a notice to passersby that hardware is available at the store.

A small window was done as a table setting with an LP—a "platter" instead of a platter—at the center. This was a display of "dinner music," according to the caption. The record and the silver service were both for sale at the store, and the window showed an extreme

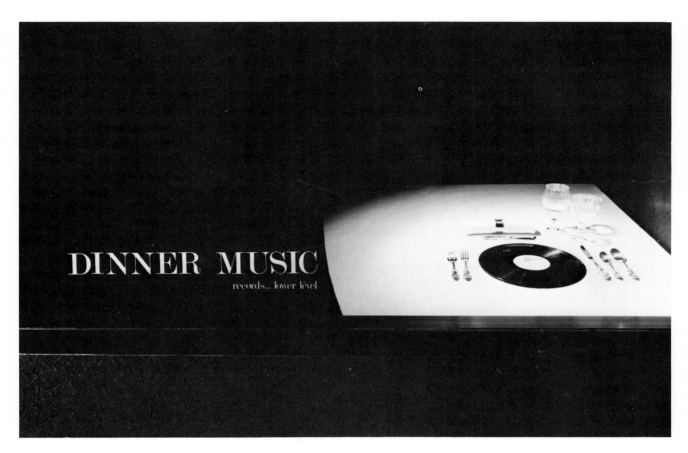

DINNER MUSIC
records... lower level

economy of design—each object serving as the others' ornament or illustration—that is often a quality of good display work. A display done in a standard, room-sized window consisted of a table and chairs and a china cabinet all solidly planted in the middle of a makeshift enclosure of half-finished walls, carpenter's tools, and measures. "Furniture to build a room around," the window copy read.

Sign work, especially for window captions, is itself a main element of Nelson's displays. Much of the written copy is painted onto the window glass or on lucite boards hung inside the windows. The calligraphy or printing becomes an element of the overall design, and there is something about this technique that seems very "contemporary"—perhaps it carries the concept of white space in graphic design a step further by, in effect, erasing the empty areas altogether, while superimposing the written image as a further "layer" of design. There is in any case an elegance in this way of handling window signage, stemming partly from the economy of an artful grafting of design onto design and partly from the quality of the work itself.

Nelson keeps up with display and fashion trends in New York, California, and Europe, and in developing his own style and ideas, he regards his windows in part as laboratories in which to combine and experiment with what he has learned from these and other sources. The result is display work that is highly distinctive rather than eclectic in any patchwork sense. At a store that prides itself on its "pioneering spirit," ZCMI's current display work must be considered among its genuine achievements.

Ron Nelson, ZCMI, Salt Lake City. Record display by designer Brent Erklens, 1977. Photograph by Hal Rumel. Courtesy ZCMI.

RAYMOND MASTROBUONI

Because fine jewelry is so much more expensive than most other types of merchandise, the purpose of a display in which it is shown is, according to Raymond Mastrobuoni, vice president and director of visual merchandising and store planning for Cartier, Inc., necessarily somewhat different from that of most other displays. One jeweler on Fifth Avenue, for example, usually places only a small, straightforward color photograph or display of unusual gemstones in each display window, and this, Mastrobuoni says, makes the store look forbidding to most passersby. It encourages only serious buyers to enter, which is almost certainly the management's intention. If so, then the windows are very effective in the store's terms and point to the fact that a window display may repel as well as attract passersby, intentionally or otherwise, while also attempting to promote sales.

Cartier's windows are mainly intended to further public relations, to "keep the store's name circulating," Mastrobuoni says. Although the jewelry shown in the windows is chosen by a buyer with sales in mind, it is assumed that few passersby will buy on impulse from the store's windows. The displays are viewed more as free shows that may make the store more inviting to passersby who are potential customers and who might not otherwise stop at the store if not for the windows.

A survey taken soon after Mastrobuoni became display director showed that about 25 percent of Cartier's customers do enter the store out of an interest in the windows. Usually the items purchased are not the ones displayed in the windows, but less expensive ones. The survey also showed that about as many people come into the store in response to the windows as to print advertising. Since ads are generally many times more expensive to produce than a display is, the survey, which Mastrobuoni conducted and which involved a simple procedure of having customers fill out a brief questionnaire, indicated the relatively high sales-effectiveness of the windows. Management, as is still often the case, was surprised by the finding and gave Mastrobuoni an unlimited budget for the New York store's displays.

Although almost any object in a window display can be made to look expensive, Mastrobuoni thinks that this is not necessarily the effect of a well-designed window. At a book store that he has noticed, for instance, several copies of a single book are shown in the windows in a graphically pleasing arrangement. No costly props are used. There is nothing elaborate or pretentious in the style or handling of the windows to suggest that the price range of books sold there may be higher than at another store. The displays show a feeling for intelligent design, which a larger and larger audience, Mastrobuoni thinks, is aware of and appreciates.

With respect to a relatively simple and attractive style of display that may be applied to almost any type of shop merchandise, Mastrobuoni thinks that American displaymen can probably learn a great deal from their Japanese counterparts and from Japanese culture generally. A concern for harmony and design is apparent in so many aspects of Japanese daily life and culture—in the settings of the meditation gardens, in the way restaurant food is arranged on a plate—and similar ideas about form and pattern are seen in many contemporary Japanese windows. In a Japanese display in which cameras were shown against a paper background of traditional pattern brocade, for instance, relatively old and recent works of design have been related with surprising effect. Mastrobuoni, as did Gene McCabe, under whom he originally worked at Cartier, has tried to combine traditional decorative elements with distinctly modern ones in his windows.

The size and shape of Cartier's windows are varied with each display, once every two weeks, by means of decorative maskings over the inner window glass. The window openings are approximately 3 by 4 feet (.9 by 1.2 meters), but for most displays are masked down to openings of a few inches square. The maskings call attention to the windows from a distance, like posters, and regular passersby take them as a signal that a new set of windows has been installed. They have been done in metal relief work, as painted floral designs, as portholes, and with electrocardiograms. Considered as architectural ornaments along a major city street, the maskings are noted by passersby for the very fact that they are regularly changed.

Ideas for windows come from many sources. While visiting Japan, Mastrobuoni studied origami with a Japanese kindergarten class and went to a Buddhist monastery to learn flower arranging. When his wife lost a ring down the kitchen sink, this became the idea for a set of windows.

Mastrobuoni is interested in cameras and in general by light as it can be transformed into various visual effects or illusions. He likes to display silver and crystal on mirrored surfaces on which they appear to float or hover. He has experimented with holography for his windows, a technique that he says has now become inexpensive enough to be used by many stores. For large-scale windows, light can be used, he says, instead of a background wall, if rows of spotlights are installed and aimed straight down just behind the window floor. If the spots are squared off, covered with a dark gel, possibly a dark blue, and spaced

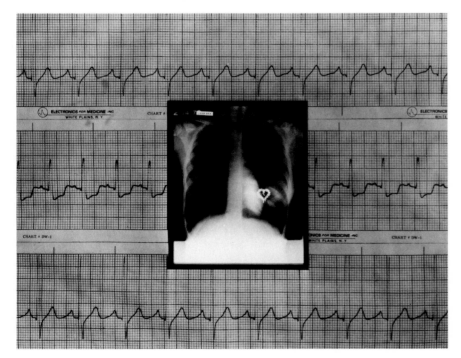

X-ray window, Raymond Mastrobuoni, Cartier, Inc., New York, 1974. Photograph by Malan Studio, Inc., New York. Courtesy Malan Studio, Inc., New York.

close enough so that the beams just overlap, the effect would be of a shimmering wall of light, backing the display.

Humor has sometimes arisen out of his interest in light, as when Mastrobuoni sent a woman wearing a heart-shaped pin from the store to have a chest x-ray. The technician asked the woman to remove the pin, but when she replied that she never went anywhere without her jewelry, the x-ray was made, with the outline of the heart—as Mastrobuoni had planned—showing on top of the subject's ribcage. The x-ray, mounted on white lucite board just inside the window glass and lighted from behind with an even fluorescent light, became the display of the pin.

For a set of Christmas windows, Mastrobuoni used two-way mirrors inside the window glass, with the window side of the mirrors facing outward. On the rear wall of each window he had a standard reflecting mirror, setting up a tunnel of infinite reflections at the center of which had been placed a candle, various seasonal ornaments, and lights. Mastrobuoni varies his displays considerably, but is especially interested in such visual effects. The appeal of such windows is not just that of a technological accomplishment, although his displays of state of the art techniques contribute to the making of a contemporary image for the store.

ROBERT CURRIE

It is a curious cultural fact that male display mannequins are, almost without exception, nowhere nearly as graceful or realistic in appearance as are their female counterparts. The best female mannequins have uncanny presence in a window. They are remarkably lifelike in their modeling and poses. The male figures, by contrast, often appear to be ill or in pain. What is more, most passersby are apparently so unused to seeing male figures in a window display and so few of the poses used seem even remotely believable that, according to Robert Currie, "It's very hard to put half a dozen male mannequins in a window without it looking like a gay bar."

While display director at Henri Bendel during the early seventies, Currie liked to use a grouping of female figures, each one dressed and made up to suggest a different type that passersby might identify with. But for Andre Oliver, a New York men's shop where Currie has recently been designing the windows, he has had the features of the male figures' heads removed, reducing them to an abstraction, and has painted the mannequins over in the store's colors. The mannequins seem to blend into the background (there is no wall separating the window space from the store interior), and the clothes stand out. This, Currie suggests plausibly, is often the way men are actually perceived in relation to their clothes: "With a man, it's the clothes that count, as far as style or fashion is concerned. The face isn't considered nearly as much as a woman's is. Most male mannequins for this reason seem too specific. But with a woman, everything—the hair, the make-up, the whole being—is considered."

While at Bendel, Currie was largely responsible for starting a "theater of the street" or "situation" style of window display that gained sudden, wide attention for display among passersby and in the media. Just as there is more than one way to commit a murder, not all situation windows were alike or equally interesting. In fact, although situation displays were mainly publicized for their shock value and "sex-and-violence," Currie was really involved in a theater of surprise in which part of the surprise consisted of a Pop realism in the choice of stage settings. A "Winged Victory" (see page 189) or a telephone booth or a sportscar might appear in a window, or almost any other object so long as it was not an expected sight in a window display. A still more engaging surprise was the attempt by Currie to express a more than passing emotion in these windows. In a display showing a bunch of masked women going for a romp in their nightgowns, a basic feeling about the need to cover human nakedness had been touched on—among other things! And the very fact that this scene was presented in the publicly exposed and obviously commercial setting of a display window lent added pathos to a drama about intimacy and mixed emotion.

Currie's "violent" windows at Bendel resembled Alfred Hitchcock's violence, in that Currie never actually showed the victim's blood but relied more on implication for dramatic effect. The gory details, if there were any, were left for the viewer, if anyone, to imagine. Here, what Currie calls "editing," came into play: knowing what to leave out as well as what to show. "It's impossible to reproduce a supermarket inside a store window, which some people tried. But you can represent the idea of a supermarket, by just showing ten thousand bars of soap."

One week at Bendel, a mannequin was seen lying on the floor at the extreme right of the window, apparently dead, by a low table with several small bottles scattered across it. The mannequin had a bottle in her hand, its contents spilled. In the left background, three mannequins stood chatting quietly, all looking on with apparent indifference. What had gone on here? Currie explains: "It was all just an accident. The woman simply picked the wrong bottle . . . and chose death."

How appropriate, in a way, such touches of the macabre seem to display, dealing as it so often does in human effigies: the mannequin's dumb form. But Currie's windows also brought forth the drama and elegance of beautiful clothes, while also entertaining passersby who could care less about the clothes. He has found that the best displays are often those that do not seem meant to be taken quite seriously and that a very effective way of giving a "feeling of life" to a window is through the use of humor.

"If you're doing a fur window," Currie says, recalling a Bendel fur sale display, "you can't use a fox as a prop. It's the wrong idea. But I found a gorilla, and put it in the window with a mannequin in an evening dress. There was no merchandise in the window. The copy read, 'You'll go ape over our furs. . . .' Now not everyone would have gotten it. But all the furs that week sold."

To "get" that window—or another in which Currie placed a nun among a grouping of mannequins in warm weather dresses with the caption "Summer Habits"—the viewer has to unravel a play on objects and words. There was something unmistakably evil about the choice of the nun. The gorilla as part of a Beauty-and-the-Beast team was deadpan confection. In both displays, words were used to give the objects in the window an added sense—added *presence*. And giving presence to an object is the essence of dramatic display. Ironically, for

"Summer Habits," Robert Currie, Henri Bendel, Inc., New York, mid-1970s. Photograph by Bill Bernardo, Jr. Courtesy Robert Currie.

a medium that is often associated with sophisticated fashions, display, if it is an art, is a primitive art in that the presence of an object is all-important to it.

Currie refers to display as "disposable art," an apt enough description of the medium at any time, but one which, like the situation windows themselves, has special Pop connotations. He feels that the time of the situation window has definitely passed, and although he does not see very much current work that strikes him as remarkable, he is generally pleased by the trend away from reliance on "the prop," a display style that he associates especially with the fifties.

Most beautiful clothes, according to Currie, do not need elaborate settings in a display to attract customers. Displayed clearly, the clothes sell themselves. Once at Bendel, Currie was given clothes to display that were not as exciting as usual: "So I camouflaged them," he says, "in a birch forest in the window. And all the clothes sold." Let the buyer, beware. But another time, three exquisite dresses stayed on the rack at Bendel a long time. "People somehow couldn't see the idea of the dress when it was on the hanger. But when they were put on figures in the window, without elaborate propping, the three dresses sold almost immediately."

Currie considers himself an artist, and he sees no contradiction in the idea that a work of art can have a selling function. While display can be an art, he says, only a few displaymen are artists, and this is not necessarily a bad thing. Not everyone wants to have to think about a store window when they go shopping, or to be "moved" by one, or for that matter, to be made to laugh. It depends on the types of customers the store is trying to attract. Insofar as a display is a work of art, Currie says, the window has a double audience: the store's potential customers and other passersby who may also find it odd, entertaining, beautiful, or surprising.

During the two years, beginning in January 1976, that he was display director of Bonwit Teller, Colin Birch made what were among the most intelligently realized and adventurous graphic statements seen in New York display. Few displaymen responded as decisively as did Birch to the need to find a simpler, more merchandise-oriented style of presentation than the situation style of the early seventies. Birch, who had previously been interior display manager at Saks Fifth Avenue under Henry F. Callahan and who now directs his own consulting firm, worked out a poster-clear attitude toward the use of what he has considered the most basic material in window display: the space itself.

At Bonwit Teller, Birch removed dividers between adjacent windows along each main bank of the Fifth Avenue store. Relatively large blocs of interconnecting display space were thus carved out for use. Moldings and frames were also eliminated, making the exposed glass wider and higher. Window floors, walls, and sides, Birch decided, would be lined for most weeks with semireflective white vinyl on fitted panels. Matte solid-color vinyl, with its sleek surface clarity and cleanness of finish, has been one of the characteristic background materials of the mid- and late seventies. By using white, Birch heightened the feeling of spaciousness that is a key to the visual drama of his architectural style of display.

Birch in his windows played upon the fact of contemporary city life that space is a luxury in itself. Leaving the windows nearly empty thus became for him a gesture of extravagance.

Birch typically used only one or two mannequins in a window, usually placed to the side to make passersby have to look a little bit to find the figure. In some windows, the mannequins in nearby windows were posed to seem aware of each other, building a dramatic interest for the displays without the aid (and expense) of elaborate stage settings. With various props—rows of plastic pennants, large paper lanterns, bands of solid color vinyl extended from window to window—visual, broad-canvas effects were achieved that were decorative, boldly scaled, and at times quite surprising. In this way, the literal window space was left intact instead of being overlaid with a theatrical illusion. More attention was concentrated on the clothes.

During the day, the white vinyl surfaces reflected natural daylight, in effect working as an element of the display lighting system rather than merely as its container. Awnings, used at most stores to decrease the sun's reflectance on the window glass, were considered more of an obstruction by Birch and were not used. Lighting was designed mainly for night-viewing. And at night the white surfaces served as screens across which patterns of reflecting colored light were highly visible.

As Bonwit Teller's unofficial fashion director, Birch went to the market with the store's buyers to choose from each new fashion collection. He also decided, unlike most display directors, exactly what clothes would go in the windows and in what colors. This allowed him to plan the displays with an especially close knowledge of the merchandise. Often an idea for a set of windows would occur to him at the showings when the mood of the new fashion season first becomes apparent. A showing, however, might be six months in advance of the window installation, and Birch usually left final details unsettled until the last few weeks or days so as to have the windows convey a mood for

COLIN BIRCH

*Bicentennial display by Colin Birch,
Bonwit Teller, New York, 1976.
Photograph by Jerry P. Melmed.
Courtesy Jerry P. Melmed.*

the clothes with the freshness of an improvisation.

Unlike display directors at many large stores, Birch did not spend, or believe in spending, much money on each set of windows. Windows are temporary and should, he felt, reflect that reality. At Bonwit Teller he considered lavish theatricality unnecessarily distracting in a window display. He typically chose props with which a mood or attitude towards the clothes might be rapidly suggested, but without seriously competing with the clothes for attention.

Large pine cones densely scattered across the white vinyl-lined floors were the only propping used for a set of fall fashion displays, and a few weeks later, he relined the windows with burlap and used arrangements of burlap sacks filled with walnuts as the settings for figures in quilt-and-burlap coats and dresses. Birch once arranged pressed silk flowers on the window glass, leaving the white walls as background absolutely bare, with mannequins in between, in an atmosphere of extreme airiness, light, and seasonal charm (see page 201).

Birch, who had overall responsibility for window and interior display at all Bonwit Teller stores, spent much of his display budget on custom-designed mannequins and on tools and equipment. Most props were made in the store's workshop by a full-time carpenter-craftsman, and this resulted in substantial savings over the cost of ordering similar work from display houses. Birch considered the ready-made props and screens that display manufacturers typically offer to be false notes for the type of display he was designing at Bonwit Teller. For his purposes, he would have liked display houses to serve as central suppliers of basic materials—bricks, tiles, sand, vinyls, live and artificial plants, lumber, fabrics, papers—all things that he used often and had to spend time shopping for.

For most purposes, Birch preferred at Bonwit Teller to use abstract mannequins. The figures allowed the clothes to be seen on a sculptural form that leaves the wearer's identity a little ambiguous, to be decided by the viewer. Age, for instance, is often an important consideration in choosing clothes. As selling agents, the abstract mannequins might appeal to the widest possible audience. At Bonwit's, Birch used more realistic, fully made-up figures mainly when displaying junior fashions for customers 16 to 21. His assumption was that a woman of that age has not yet formed a complete image of herself and is still looking for models that present a ready-made picture. For Bonwit's men's clothing displays, Birch favored abstract mannequins, but did not find a really satisfactory design on the market.

While composition and choice of materials are always important in window display, they were especially so in severely abstract windows such as Birch's, which would otherwise have looked like small assortments, not of select goods, but of extraneous details.

Variety from week to week is also essential. As an experiment, Birch once placed nearly identical groupings of mannequins in each window along the Fifth Avenue window banks (see page 200). The mannequins were similarly posed. Each had on clothes by a different designer. Designers were identified by photo-and-lettering captions on the window floors and across the lower portion of the glass. This graphic series of multiple takes was thoroughly original as window display and worked well from a merchandising standpoint, since an unusually large amount of the store's clothes had been shown in one sweep.

Birch had weekly reports made on the amount of sales of merchandise displayed in the windows. In general, the correlation was quite high. The extreme economy of Birch's extravagant style perhaps reflected a more business-minded atmosphere in display in the mid-seventies as well as Birch's personal aesthetic. His windows at Bonwit Teller were a designer's paradox. He had put twice as much, if not more, merchandise in the store's windows than had been seen in them previously, and the windows, he was pleased to observe, still looked empty.

MAGGIE SPRING

Violets became the emblem and a part of the signature of Bonwit Teller in New York during the 1940s, when the flowers first appeared in an exquisite watercolor illustration on the Bonwit Teller shopping bag. At that time, silk violets were also offered to the store's customers.

Early in 1978, violets, which have remained on Bonwit's graphics, also began to appear here and there around the Fifth Avenue store's ground floor interiors and, oddly but delicately, in a series of window displays in which violets sprouted from the branches of trees.

The windows were by Maggie Spring, Bonwit Teller's display director for the first half of 1978. Her interest in the store's decorative tradition is part of a larger interest in working with visual elements of "the old and the new" in displays that relate the store's new clothes to standards of elegance in fashion and design that do not become dated.

A mannequin that Spring helped plan for the store was designed in part from photographs of thirties and forties Bonwit Teller displays. Another source for the design of the figure was forties Hollywood glamor portraits. The mannequin was posed for by a young fashion model, who also appears in the store's photo advertisements. A new image of the Bonwit Teller woman was thus formed and presented in a well-coordinated way by Spring and others responsible for the store's various forms of advertising and promotion.

In placing the mannequins in the windows, Spring usually had each one stand individually, rather than in groups or in situations in which they seem to be aware of each other. This, she says, is the way that a self-confident woman usually wants to present herself when she walks into a room. It is a form of display in everyday life. In the windows, the mannequin and clothes became the center of the viewer's interest.

Spring preferred to make the background in her windows a little indistinct, or atmospheric, in order to have its presence felt, but not as a distraction. In one series, tall standing Japanese painted screens lent continuity and an antique quality of light to the windows. Light, in another series, was projected on the window walls as phases of the moon, with tree branches peering out here and there from around the window frames as additional bits of stage-setting. Once, murals were painted on the window walls (see page 203), and for Valentine's Day the window glass itself was frosted down to heart-shaped openings.

Large blocs of space were left unfilled in the windows each week as part of the overall graphic effect of the displays. And while often the decor for a series of displays tied together a complete window bank in a single continuous pattern, the placement of the mannequins and other details set each window off from those adjacent to it. Spring compares the impression that she wanted each display to give to that of a still life in an elegant magazine.

Before designing her first windows at Charles Jourdan in New York in 1975, Maggie Spring had worked at Bonwit Teller, first as a saleswoman, then as a store manager, assistant buyer, assistant fashion coordinator, and buyer. Just prior to becoming display director at Jourdan, she had done publicity work for the designer Ralph Lauren and, altogether, had an unusually wide variety of merchandising experience as background for display. As a display director, she has always been very aware of the type of customer the store that she works for and her windows are likely to attract.

Maggie Spring, Bonwit Teller, New York, 1978. Photograph by Jerry P. Melmed. Courtesy Jerry P. Melmed.

At most shoe stores, the windows are displayed as straightforward catalogs, an arrangement that seems appropriate for sensible walking shoes. As design, such shoe windows have more to do with marching than with dancing. But at Charles Jourdan, which has been known as a leading designer and seller of fashion shoes, Spring used the windows as a stage. Candy Pratts, as display director from 1970 to 1975, had done so before her. To Spring, shoes in pairs became actors and actresses, with imaginary people in them.

A few props implied a situation—shoes saluting the flag, shoes looking in at a caged beast, shoes caged like a beast, a crowd of shoes gathered on a bridge where a young woman had apparently stepped out of her shoes for the last time in an act of passionate desperation (see page 193), and so on. Often, there was humor. And in some windows, Spring made the design more abstract to vary the feeling of the displays from week to week. She took advantage of the unusually large size of the windows (6 to 7 feet deep, about 6 feet high, and 10 and 13 feet wide) [1.6 to 2.2 meters deep, about 1.6 meters high, and 3 and 4 meters wide] for graphic effects, with neon cabaret figures in one series and large fantasy airplanes in another. Heads turned on passing buses, as well as among pedestrians, to see the Jourdan windows.

Works of art were often borrowed for a display. This practice had been started before Spring came to Jourdan. It worked well for the artists, who had a chance to have their work seen, as well as for the store. Spring's windows were done with wonderful taste and with insight into design that applied equally in the handling of the shoes and the art. The windows added to the store's own reputation for design, becoming an identification, a face for the store that many passersby remembered.

The Bonwit Teller violets have been part of that store's identification since the forties. Once while Spring and her staff were working in the window, there was a tapping on the glass. A woman on the sidewalk was holding up a delicately made silk violet, pinned to her muff, for them to see. "This is the original Bonwit Teller violet!" she spoke visibly. Her voice did not carry through the glass. "I got it here 35 years ago!" Maggie Spring and the woman on the street were both delighted.

Elegance and beauty are qualities in fashion and in windows that Spring feels Bonwit Teller's customers especially appreciate and which seem appropriate to her now for display. Elegance and beauty are both lasting values—classics. This is the light in which Spring presented Bonwit Teller's clothes.

PLATES

1 *Marshall Field & Co., Chicago*
Arthur V. Fraser, 1930

2   Franklin-Simon, New York
Norman Bel Geddes, 1929

3

4

3–4   Lord & Taylor, New York
Dana O'Clare, 1935 or 1936

5   Lord & Taylor, New York
Dana O'Clare, 1932

6

7

8

9

10

11

10   Bonwit Teller, New York
Tom Lee, 1938

11   Bonwit Teller, New York
Tom Lee, 1938 or 1939

12   Bonwit Teller, New York
Tom Lee, 1940

13

14

15

13–14   Bonwit Teller, New York
Tom Lee, 1938

15   Bonwit Teller, New York
Edward Ballinger, early 1940s
Designer: Salvador Dali

16   *Saks Fifth Avenue, New York*
Sidney Ring, 1942 or 1943

17   *The Emporium, San Francisco*
Display director unknown, 1934

18   *Saks Fifth Avenue, Beverly Hills*
California
Jim Buckley, 1940

16

17

19   *Marshall Field & Co., Chicago*
Display staff, 1948

20   *Carson Pirie Scott & Co., Chicago*
Clement Bradley, 1948

21

22

23

24

24, 26 *Lord & Taylor, New York*
Henry F. Callahan, 1953

25 *Lord & Taylor, New York*
Henry F. Callahan, 1954

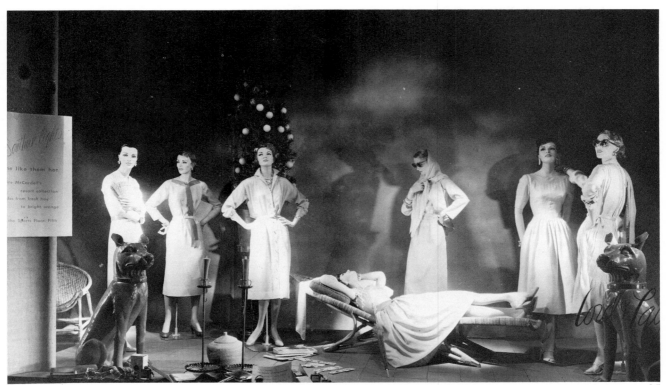

25

26

28

27   Marshall Field & Co., Chicago
Display staff, 1956

28   Bonwit Teller, New York
Gene Moore, 1949

29   30

31   32

33

29   Bonwit Teller, New York
Gene Moore, 1951
Topiary horse and rider: Jeanne Owens

30   Bonwit Teller, New York
Gene Moore, 1957
Bentwood sculpture: Stan Vanderbeek

31   Bonwit Teller, New York
Gene Moore, 1957

32   Bonwit Teller, New York
Gene Moore, 1951

33   Bonwit Teller, New York
Gene Moore, 1956

34

34–35 *Bonwit Teller, New York*
Gene Moore, 1950
Background photographs: Gene Moore

36 *Bonwit Teller, New York*
Gene Moore, 1950
Designers: Jasper Johns,
Robert Rauschenberg

35

37 38

39 40

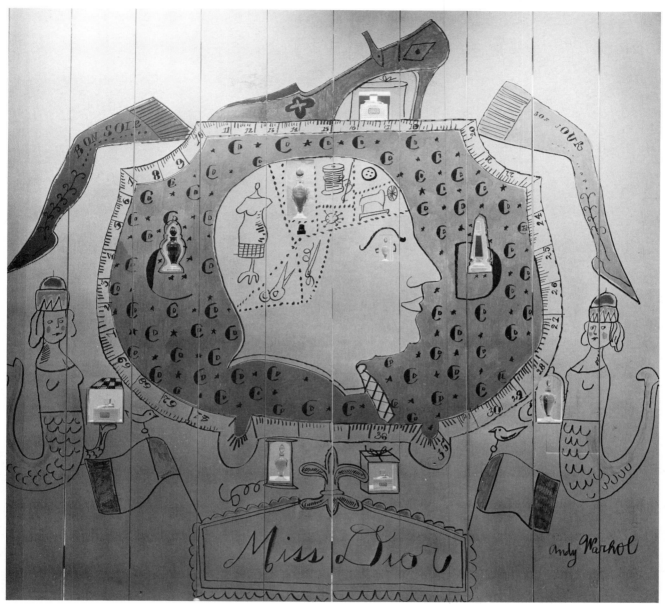

37   *Delman Shoe Salon, New York*
Gene Moore, 1941
Background: Arthur Long

38   *Bergdorf Goodman, New York*
Tom Lee, early 1950s

39   *Bonwit Teller, New York*
Gene Moore, 1947
Background: Arthur Long

40   *Bonwit Teller, New York*
Gene Moore, 1956
Designer: Jac Venza

41   *Bonwit Teller, New York*
Gene Moore, 1957
Designer: Andy Warhol

42

43

42 *Henri Bendel, Inc., New York*
Laurence B. Bartscher, late 1950s
Photograph from Window Display, *Vol. 2,*
Walter Herdeg, The Graphis Press,
Zurich, Switzerland

43 *Bergdorf Goodman, New York*
Tom Lee, early 1950s

44 *Hattie Carnegie, New York*
Howard Nevelow, 1958

45

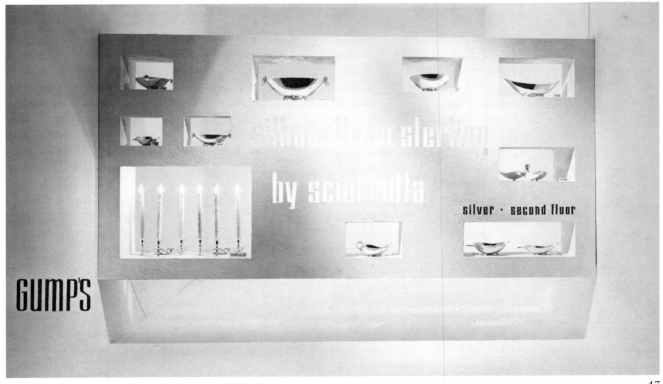

45   Gump's, San Francisco
Herb Renaud, 1952

46   Gump's, San Francisco
James H. Stearns, 1961 or 1962

47   Gump's, San Francisco
Robert J. Mahoney, mid-1960s

48

49

130

48   Gump's, San Francisco
Herb Renaud, 1951

49   Gump's, San Francisco
Leo Kenney, 1957

50   Gump's, San Francisco
Leo Kenney, late 1950s

51   Gump's, San Francisco
Al Proom, 1958
Designers: Al Proom, James H. Stearns

50

51

GUMP'S

52

53
54

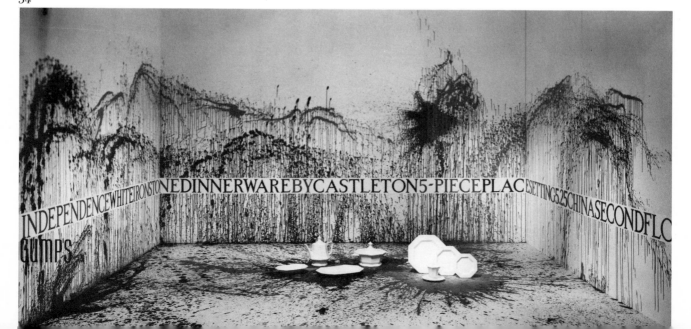

INDEPENDENCEWHITEIRONSTONEDINNERWAREBYCASTLETON5-PIECEPLACESETTING525CHINASECONDFLC

GUMP'S

55

52   Gump's, San Francisco
James H. Stearns, 1961 or 1962
Designers: James H. Stearns, Jean Dolmans

53   Gump's, San Francisco
Robert J. Mahoney, 1963
Designer: Jim Nunes

54   Gump's, San Francisco
James H. Stearns, 1961 or 1962

55   Gump's, San Francisco
James H. Stearns, 1961–1962
Designers: James H. Stearns, Jean Dolmans,
Robert J. Mahoney, Jim Nunes

56

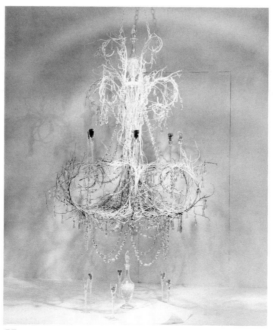

57

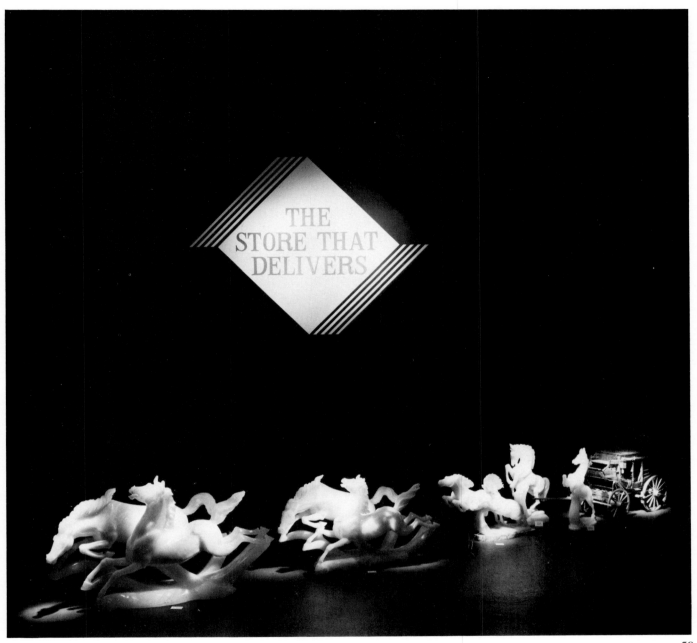

56   *Gump's, San Francisco*
Leo Kenney, mid- or late 1950s
Designers: Leo Kenney, Jean Dolmans

57   *Gump's, San Francisco*
James H. Stearns, 1963

58   *Gump's, San Francisco*
Robert J. Mahoney, 1968

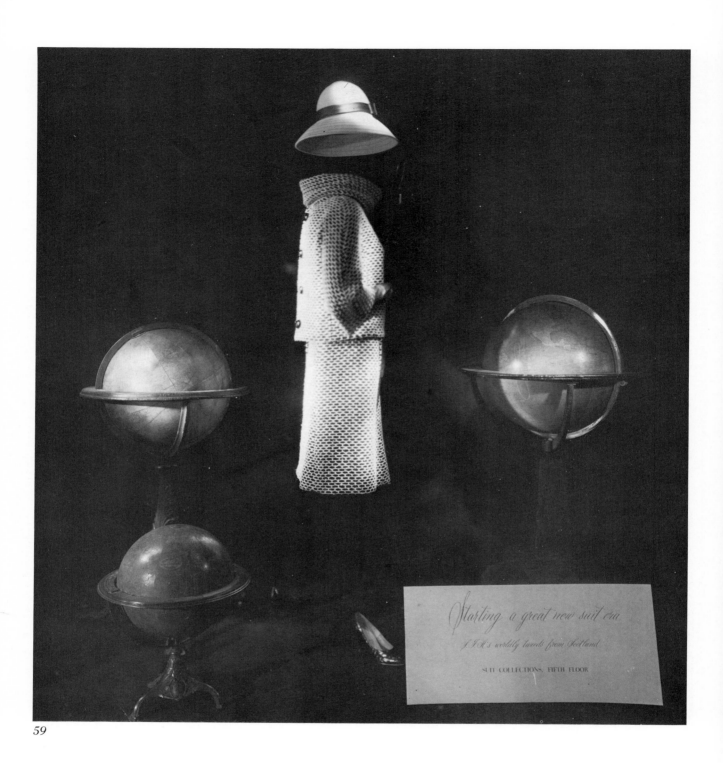

59

59 *Saks Fifth Avenue, New York*
Henry F. Callahan, 1963

60 *Saks Fifth Avenue, New York*
Henry F. Callahan, 1966

SAKS FIFTH AVENUE

61

61–62 *Saks Fifth Avenue, New York*
Henry F. Callahan, 1966

62

63   *Saks Fifth Avenue, New York*
Henry F. Callahan, 1966

64   Saks Fifth Avenue, New York
Henry F. Callahan, 1970

65

66

65 *Lord & Taylor, New York*
Paul Vogler, 1962

66 *Lord & Taylor, New York*
William Foxall Mac Elree, Jr., 1967

67

68

67　*Lord & Taylor, New York*
William Foxall Mac Elree, Jr., 1971

68　*Lord & Taylor, New York*
William Foxall Mac Elree, Jr., 1970

69   Tiffany & Co., New York
Gene Moore, 1970
Assistant: Ron Smith
Castle construction: Mark Fenyo

70   Tiffany & Co., New York
Gene Moore, 1965
Assistant: Ron Smith
Sculpture: Sam Gallo

71

72

71   *Tiffany & Co., New York*
Gene Moore, 1965
Assistant: Ron Smith
Sculpture: Sam Gallo

72   *Tiffany & Co., New York*
Gene Moore, 1969
Assistant: Ron Smith

73   *Tiffany & Co., New York*
Gene Moore, 1967
Assistant: Ron Smith

73

74

74 *Tiffany & Co., New York*
Gene Moore, 1970
Assistant: Ron Smith
Zoo: Virginia Bascomb

75 *Tiffany & Co., New York*
Gene Moore, 1970
Assistant: Ron Smith

76   *Tiffany & Co., New York*
Gene Moore, 1968
Assistant: Ron Smith
Dartboard: Karen Smith

77   *Tiffany & Co., New York*
Gene Moore, 1966
Assistant: Ron Smith

78

78   *Tiffany & Co., New York*
Gene Moore, 1967
Assistant: Ron Smith
Papier-mâché: Bill O'Connor

79   *Tiffany & Co., New York*
Gene Moore, 1970
Assistant: Ron Smith

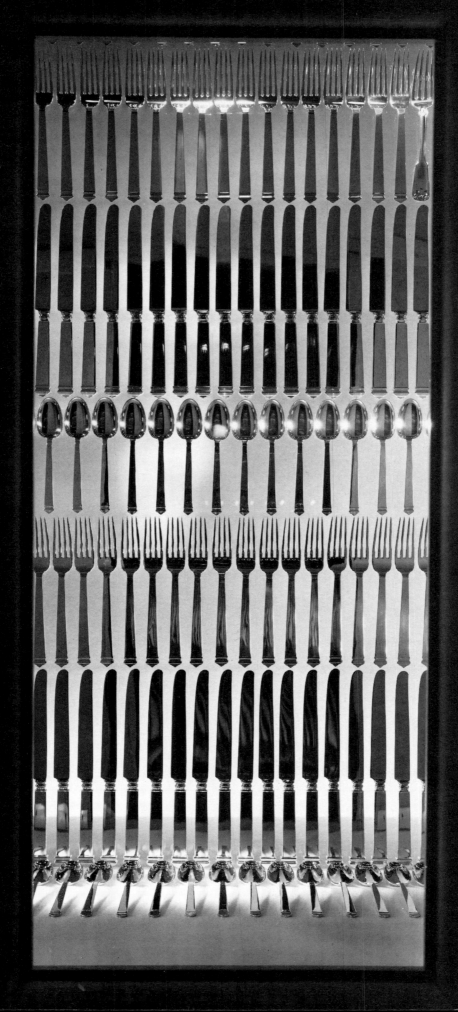

80   *Bonwit Teller, New York*
Dan Arje, 1971

81 *Bonwit Teller, New York*
Dan Arje, 1967

82

83

82 *Delman Shoe Salon, New York*
Howard Nevelow, 1970

83 *Delman Shoe Salon, New York*
Howard Nevelow, 1963

84 *Delman Shoe Salon, New York*
Howard Nevelow, 1965

85 *Delman Shoe Salon, New York*
Howard Nevelow, 1963

84

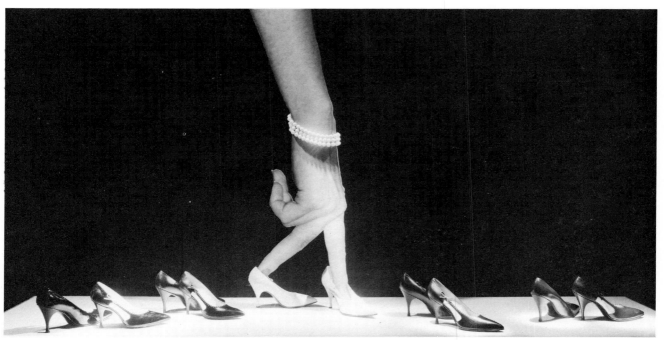

85

86

87

86 *Delman Shoe Salon, New York*
Howard Nevelow, 1968

87 *"The Castle of the Pyrenees,"*
René Magritte, 1959
Copyright A.D.A.G.P.
Private collection, New York
Photograph by G. D. Hackett Photography
Copyright G. D. Hackett Photography

88 *Delman Shoe Salon, New York*
Howard Nevelow, 1965

89

89–90   *Delman Shoe Salon, New York*
Howard Nevelow, 1962

90

91 *Delman Shoe Salon, New York*
Howard Nevelow, 1967
Assemblage: George Pfiffner

92–94 *Delman Shoe Salon, New York*
Howard Nevelow, 1972

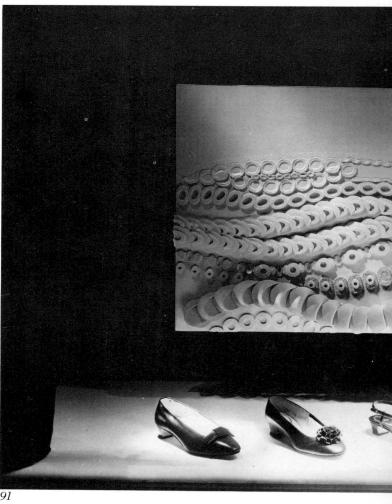

91

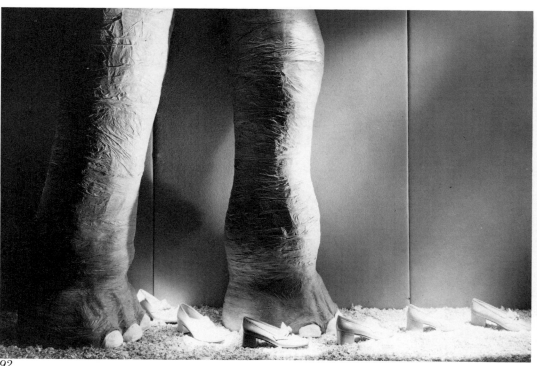

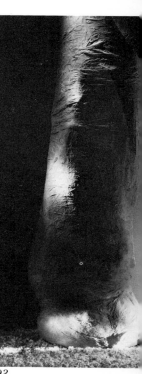

92

93

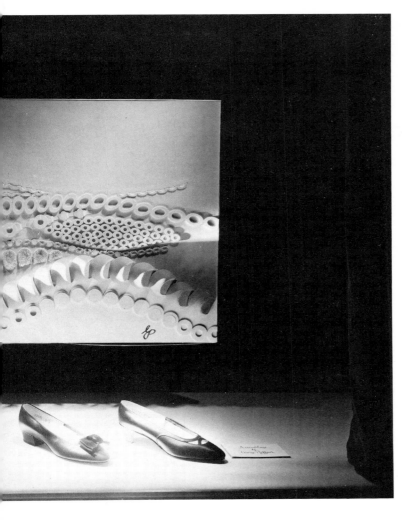

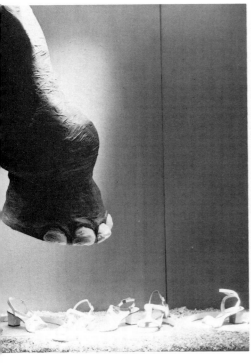

94

95

95–96   *Ohrbach's, New York*
Gene McCabe, 1960

97

98

97–100 *Ohrbach's, New York*
Gene McCabe, 1962

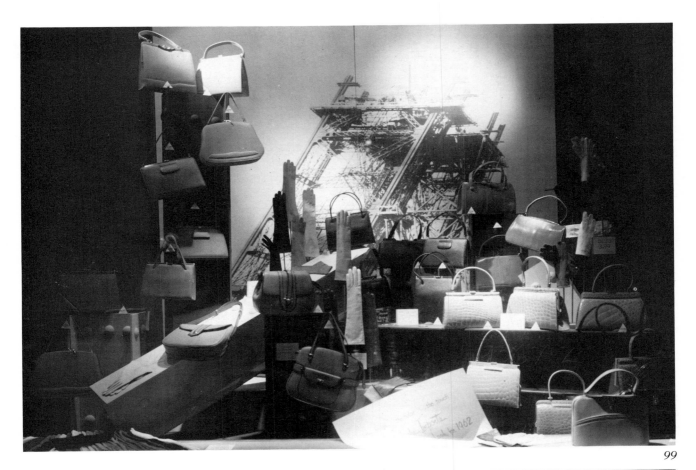

99

100

101

101–102   *Cartier, Inc., New York*
Gene McCabe, 1969
Assistant: Raymond Mastrobuoni

103

103   *Cartier, Inc., New York*
Gene McCabe, 1969
Assistant: Raymond Mastrobuoni

104   *B. Altman & Co., New York*
Robert Benzio, 1975

105

105–106   *Saks Fifth Avenue, New York*
Robert Benzio, 1977

107

108

107   Saks Fifth Avenue, New York
Robert Benzio, 1976

108   Lord & Taylor, New York
Emil A. Blasberg, 1977

109

109   D.H. Holmes Company, Ltd., New Orleans
Jerry Thorne, 1974

110–111   Lord & Taylor, New York
William Foxall Mac Elree, Jr., 1968

112   Lord & Taylor, New York
William Foxall Mac Elree, Jr., 1972

110

111
112

113

114

115

113   *Ohrbach's, New York*
Gene McCabe, 1956

114   *Lord & Taylor, New York*
Emil A. Blasberg, 1977

115   *Cartier, Inc., New York*
Raymond Mastrobuoni, 1974

116   *Cartier, Inc., New York*
Raymond Mastrobuoni, 1976

117   Cartier, Inc., New York
Raymond Mastrobuoni, 1976
Assistant: Michael Daddario

118

118–119   *Charles Jourdan Shoes, New York*
Candy Pratts, 1973

119

121

120   *Bergdorf Goodman, New York*
Jack Quinn, 1976

121   *I. Miller Shoes, New York*
Jerry Miller, 1973

122

123

186

124

122 *Bloomingdale's, New York*
Candy Pratts, 1978
Photograph by Willo Font

123 *Bloomingdale's, New York*
Candy Pratts, 1976
Photograph by Jerry P. Melmed

124 *Steuben Glass, New York*
Pat Weisberg, 1975

125 *Bloomingdale's, New York*
Candy Pratts, 1977
Photograph by Jerry P. Melmed

125

126 127
128 129

130

126   I. Magnin, San Francisco
Tom Nicoll, 1977
Photograph by Ivan Essayan Photographs

127   Bloomingdale's, New York
Candy Pratts, 1976
Photograph by Jerry P. Melmed

128   Charles Jourdan Shoes, New York
Maggie Spring, 1976
Photograph by Jerry P. Melmed
Courtesy Jerry P. Melmed

129   Henri Bendel, Inc., New York
Robert Currie, 1974

130   Henri Bendel, Inc., New York
Robert Currie, 1976
Photograph by Jerry P. Melmed
Courtesy Jerry P. Melmed

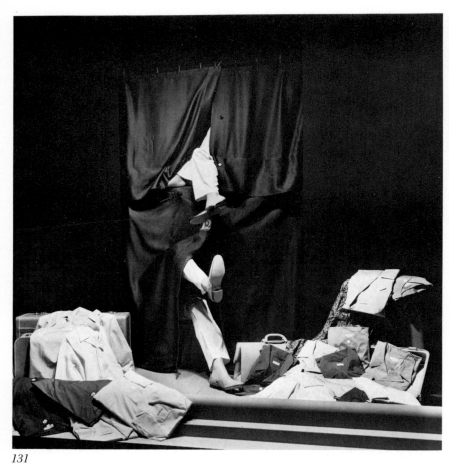

131

132

190

133

134

135

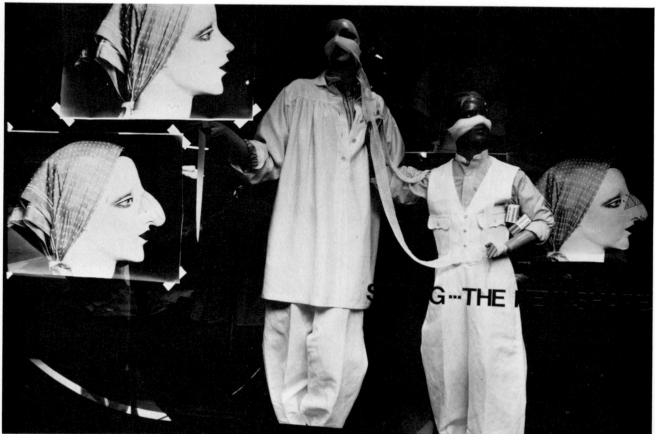

136

192

137

135   *Henri Bendel, Inc., New York*
Robert Currie, 1974

136   *San Francisco Clothing, New York*
David M. O'Grady, 1976
Photograph by John Peden

137   *Charles Jourdan Shoes, New York*
Maggie Spring, 1976
Setting: Guy Fery
Photograph by Jerry P. Melmed

138

138–139   *ZCMI, Salt Lake City, Utah*
Ron Nelson, 1977
Designer: Mike Stephens
Photographs by Hal Rumel

139

140 *ZCMI, Salt Lake City, Utah*
Ron Nelson, 1977
Designer: Jutta Gellersen
Photograph by Hal Rumel

141 *ZCMI, Salt Lake City, Utah*
Ron Nelson, 1977
Designers: Dennis Wardle, Bruce Wilcox

142 *ZCMI, Salt Lake City, Utah*
Ron Nelson, 1977
Designer: Mike Stephens
Photograph by Hal Rumel

140

141

I Remember Mama
Sunday, May 8

142

197

143

144

143–144   *Liberty House, Oakland, California*
Bill Welch, 1976

145   *I. Miller Shoes, New York*
Jerry Miller, 1974

146   *Bonwit Teller, New York*
Colin Birch, 1976
Photograph by Jerry P. Melmed

147 148
149 150

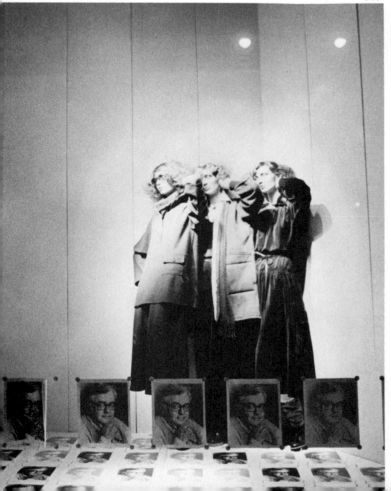

151

147–151 *Bonwit Teller, New York*
Colin Birch, 1977
Photographs by Jerry P. Melmed

PRIMAVERA FACE BY PABLO AND ELIZABETH ARDEN

153

152   *Bonwit Teller, New York*
Maggie Spring, 1978
Photograph by Jerry P. Melmed

153   *Bonwit Teller, New York*
Maggie Spring, 1978
Background: Richard Bernstein
Photograph by Jerry P. Melmed

SELECTED BIBLIOGRAPHY

Books on Display

Buckley, Jim. *The Drama of Display: Visual Merchandising and Its Techniques*. New York: Pellegrini & Cudahy, 1953.

Coutchie, Mariann. *Jewelry on Display*. Cincinnati: Signs of the Times Publishing Co., 1972.

Emory, Michael. *Windows*. Chicago: Contemporary Books, Inc., 1977.

Gaba, Lester. *The Art of Window Display*. New York & London: Studio Publications, Inc. with Crowell, 1952.

Herdeg, Walter H. (ed.). *International Window Display*. New York: Pellegrini & Cudahy, 1951.

――――. *Window Display*. Vol. 2. Zurich: The Graphis Press, 1961.

Joel, Shirley. *Fairchild's Book of Window Display*. New York: Fairchild Publications, Inc., 1973.

Kaspar, Karl (ed.), and Mickel, Liselotte. *International Window Display*. New York & Washington: Praeger, 1966.

Kiesler, Frederick. *Contemporary Art Applied to the Store and Its Display*. New York: Brentano's, 1930.

Knapp, Walter (ed.). *Schaufenster International 2 Window Display*. New York: Hastings House, Inc., 1973.

Leydenfrost, Robert J. *Window Display*. New York: Architectural Book Publishing Company, 1950.

Nonfiction

Artley, Alexandra (ed.). *The Golden Age of Shop Design*. New York: The Whitney Library of Design, 1976.

Beaton, Cecil. *Portrait of New York*. London & New York: B. T. Batsford, 1948.

Bel Geddes, Norman. *Horizons*. New York: Dover Publications, Inc., 1977.

Breuer, Marcel. *Sun and Shadow*. New York: Dodd, Mead & Company, 1955.

Dickens, Charles. *American Notes; and Pic-Nic Papers*. Philadelphia: T. B. Peterson & Brothers, 1942.

Goldwater, Robert, and D'Harnoncourt, René. *Modern Art in Your Life*. New York: The Museum of Modern Art, 1949.

Goodman, Percival, and Goodman, Paul. *Communitas: Means of Livelihood and Ways of Life*. Chicago: The Chicago University Press, 1947.

Loewy, Raymond. *Never Leave Well Enough Alone*. New York: Simon & Schuster, 1951.

Ozenfant. *Foundations of Modern Art*. New York: Dover Publications, Inc., 1952.

Purtell, Joseph. *The Tiffany Touch*. New York: Random House, 1971.

Rosebrock, Ellen Fletcher. *Counting-House Days in South Street: New York's Early Brick Seaport Buildings*. New York: South Street Seaport Museum, 1975.

Talese, Gay. *New York: A Serendipiter's Journey*. New York: Harper & Brothers, 1961.

Wiebe, Robert H. *The Search for Order, 1877–1920*. New York: Hill & Wang, 1967.

Fiction

Baum, L. Frank. *The Wonderful Wizard of Oz*. New York: Bobbs-Merrill Co., 1944.

Dickens, Charles. *The Old Curiosity Shop*. Harmondsworth, Middlesex, England: Penguin Books Ltd., 1972.

Finney, Jack. *Time and Again*. New York: Warner Paperback Library, 1971.

Lewis, Sinclair. *Main Street*. New York: The New American Library, Inc., 1961.

Periodicals

American Artist, December 1950. "Cecilia Staples," by Catherine Sullivan, pp. 52–57.

Display World, 1922–1974.

Fortune, October 1936. "Marshall Field & Company," pp. 79–87, 134–141.

Fortune, January 1949. "Show Case for Business: A Portfolio of Photographs Revealing the Strange World of Display," pp. 92–97.

Graphis, vol. 2, no. 15, 1946. "Vertès 'On Fragrance,'" by W. H. Allner, pp. 308–315.

Graphis, vol. 5, no. 26, 1949. "Cecilia Staples," by William B. McDonald, pp. 162–167.

Graphis, vol. 16, no. 92, 1960. "Gene Moore," by Tom Lee, pp. 528–533.

Life, July 12, 1937. "Grace the Dummy," pp. 32–33 and cover.

Life, Aug. 9, 1937. "The Exposition Has a 'Salon d'Elegance,'" p. 73.

Life, Dec. 13, 1937. "Life Goes to a Party," pp. 84–86.

Life, Mar. 28, 1938. "Store Window Displays Attract First-Night Enthusiasts," pp. 28–30.

The Merchants Record and Show Window, 1903–1938.

Retailing, Mar. 27, 1939. "'L'Affaire Dali' Stirs Up Debate on Art in Display," p. 12.

The Show Window, 1897–1903.

Visual Merchandising, 1974–1978.

Women's Wear Daily, Mar. 17, 1939. "Surrealist Bounces through Window of Bonwit Teller into Night Court," by Donald C. Platt, p. 40.